T0182246

Embrace your inner
PLANT LADY

Embrace your inner
PLANT ✿ LADY

EMMA BASTOW

HarperCollins*Publishers*

HarperCollins*Publishers*
1 London Bridge Street
London SE1 9GF

www.harpercollins.co.uk

HarperCollins*Publishers*
Macken House, 39/40 Mayor Street Upper
Dublin 1, D01 C9W8, Ireland

First published by HarperCollins*Publishers* 2021

10 9 8 7 6 5 4

© Emma Bastow 2021
Design by Louise Leffler

Emma Bastow asserts the moral right to be
identified as the author of this work

A catalogue record of this book is
available from the British Library

ISBN 978-0-00845496-8

Printed and bound by PNB Print, Latvia

All rights reserved. No part of this publication may be
reproduced, stored in a retrieval system, or transmitted,
in any form or by any means, electronic, mechanical,
photocopying, recording or otherwise, without the prior
written permission of the publishers.

MIX
Paper | Supporting
responsible forestry
FSC™ C007454

FSC
www.fsc.org

This book is produced from independently certified FSC™ paper
to ensure responsible forest management.

For more information visit:
www.harpercollins.co.uk/green

CONTENTS

INTRODUCTION

Welcome, plantistas, to this little book of botanical facts, houseplant hacks and a whole load of tips for keeping your plant babies happy.

Not only do houseplants purify the air we breathe, they also help to connect us to nature and are proven to reduce stress. They can also be multipurpose: turn to p.79 to discover how to turn your homegrown aloe vera into a host of beauty products, and to pp.104–27 for ideas for transforming your edible plants into delectable delights.

Perhaps you're a seasoned houseplant superstar looking for a bit of inspiration? If so, turn to 'Sensational Showstoppers' on p.42 to discover houseplant hotties to adorn your home. There you'll find profiles for ten Insta-worthy plants that any self-respecting plantfluencer would be proud to post.

Or maybe you're a newbie to this plant-parenting malarkey? No previous plant prowess needed here. 'Learn to be Green-fingered' (pp.8–29) is your quick-start guide to the basics of houseplant care, while 'Plant Matchmaking' (pp.30–41) will help you to find your perfect plant partner, taking you from apprentice to virtuoso in the turn of a page.

Fancy getting involved in the grow-your-own trend, but you're lacking outside space? Never fear – 'Eat What You Sow' (pp.104–27) shows you how to cultivate your very own kitchen-windowsill garden. In no time at all you'll be an expert grower of blow-your-socks-off chillies, sensational salad ingredients and the prettiest edible flowers.

Succulent and cacti fans will find pp.60–71 packed with information on these drought-hardy houseplants, while orchid aficionados will want to check out pp.88–103. And for any plantistas looking for guidance on essential (and not-so-essential) equipment, you'll find everything you need to know in the handy 'Kit and Kaboodle' section on pp.14–15.

Whatever your reasons for picking up this book, I hope you'll enjoy it – and may your plants be forever perky.

Emma Bastow

LEARN TO BE
GREEN-FINGERED

THE BASICS OF HOUSEPLANT CARE

Not naturally green-fingered? Concerned that your plant babies won't thrive in your care? Do not worry – even you (yes, you!) can become a green goddess with this any-fool-can-do-it guide to plant care. Just remember that, much like humans, all plants really need to grow is light, water and energy. The tricky part is balancing these to suit your shoots.

Water, water everywhere

Water little and often, right? Well, not always.

Watering, especially when to do it and how much, can get even the most experienced plant parent in a pickle. Follow these golden rules to keep your hydrangeas hydrated and your polka dots perky:

- **Do use filtered water or rainwater, if possible.** While ordinary tap water won't do any harm (unless it's softened), your plants will love the lower chlorine levels in filtered and rainwater.
- **Don't use cold or warm water.** Extremes of temperature can damage the plant's structures, so always use room-temperature water. Refilling your watering can after use and allowing it to sit until your plants need watering again is a good way to ensure the water is the right temperature.
- **Do tailor the amount of water to the type of plant.** Many people make the mistake of judging the amount of water a plant needs by its size. While this isn't necessarily wrong, always check the guidance for your individual plants – as a

general rule, plants with bigger leaves originating from tropical areas need more water than those with smaller leaves found in desert regions.
- **Don't let the leaves droop.** Try to water your plants before they start looking a little sad, as by this point their natural defences will be down, leaving them more susceptible to disease. To check if your plant needs a drink, pop your finger into the soil up to the first joint. If your finger is dry when removed, it's time to water.
- **Do soak rather than sprinkle.** Water your plants well with a suitable break between each watering. Sprinkling your plants with water daily (which many nervous waterers resort to) will mean that the water may evaporate before it reaches the roots. That said . . .
- **Don't overwater.** Too much water is more likely to kill a plant than too little, so approach the watering can with caution. Those drainage holes in the base of your pots are there for a reason and are designed to prevent the roots from becoming oxygen-deprived and rotten (see p.131 for more on this).

Let them see the light

All plants, even those suitable for low-light environments, need light to survive. No amount of feeding, nurturing and caring will change this. Without enough light, your plants can't photosynthesise (see p.139) and will become yellow and stop growing. The key here is to match the plant to the room. For example, if you're not blessed with sunlight streaming through the windows from sunrise to sunset, a jade plant (see p.24) probably isn't for you. However, you might opt for peace lilies (see p.37), which generally do very well in low-light conditions (albeit with fewer flowers than would be the case in a better-lit space). A bit of research into light requirements before purchasing a plant, or taking a cutting, will go a long way to helping your new additions to thrive.

TOO LITTLE LIGHT: if you have a plant that seems to be suffering from light deprivation, the obvious thing to do is (gradually) move it to a brighter area. However, if this isn't possible, you might want to look at getting artificial lighting (see p.15), especially during the dark winter months. Options range from inexpensive and fuss-free fluorescent light bulbs to more costly, specially designed horticultural lighting for those who are serious about bringing the light in.

TOO MUCH LIGHT: it's also possible for plants to be exposed to too much sunlight, causing burns (beige or brown patches) to appear on the leaves, much like sunburn. To fix this, either reposition the plant away from direct sunlight and follow its usual watering and fertilising routine or block out some of the light with a filter (adjustable blinds are perfect for this).

Feeding time

How and when to fertilise your plants will depend on the type of plant and the time of year, but whatever you do, don't skip this important and often overlooked step. All plants need nutrients to thrive, and potted plants have limited resources as their roots can't spread out looking for the most abundant supply. So, it's your job to provide nutrients to the soil using plant fertiliser. There are many different types on the market and an all-purpose feed is a good place to start for the first-timer.

As a rule of thumb, most houseplants need feeding about once a month in spring and summer (no need to feed in the cooler months as your plants won't be doing much growing); flowering plants will require a more frequent dosage, and how much will depend on the plant's size, so always follow the advice on the fertiliser packaging.

Kitchen scraps make a surprisingly good fertiliser for some plant types. Ground coffee, eggshells and banana peels in particular can add valuable nutrients to the soil. However, always research which types of leftovers are suitable for your particular plant, and don't be tempted to overdo it; too much of a good thing can lead to mould growth and encourage root rot – not a good look for your home.

Clean and green

Keeping your plants clean and dust-free will ensure they can photosynthesise properly and generally stay looking as perky as possible. How often you need to clean the leaves will depend on their environment, but if you can see a visible layer of dust or if a finger gently rubbed on a leaf comes away grubby, it's time for a spruce-up.

BIG ONES

Larger plants that can't be moved can easily be cleaned in situ using a soft, damp cloth and, for a heavy coating of dust or grime, they should be spritzed with water from a spray bottle filled with room-temperature water (a good tip is to fill the bottle a few hours before you intend to use it and let it stand in the same room as the plant to reach the ambient temperature). If using a water spray, simply spray the leaves from a distance so as not to damage them, then in both cases very gently wipe each leaf in turn, starting at the top and working down towards the tip, with a soft cloth or duster.

SMALL ONES

Smaller plants and those with very delicate leaves can be cleaned by inverting the plant and submerging the leafy sections into a sink filled with tepid water (again, you can allow the water to stand for a few hours to reach room temperature). Make sure you secure the soil first (wrapping a damp tea towel around the base of the plant is a good way to ensure the soil doesn't escape), then very gently submerge the plant into the water and swish it around. Allow the plant to air dry before moving it back to its regular spot.

FUZZY ONES

Plants with furry leaves, such as African violets, are more tricky to clean. The best course of action here is to prevent the dust settling in the first place by ensuring there is good air flow in the room (although no cold draughts, which your plants will object to), but if your furry-leaved friend is looking less than fresh, try teasing the dust from the leaves with a super-soft brush.

PEST PROTECTION

If you notice tiny holes in your plant's leaves, look a little closer – it may be harbouring an army of pests who are feasting on your foliage. The simplest way to bid farewell to bugs is to treat your plant with neem oil. This antibacterial oil is non-toxic to the plant and friendly insects (bees and ladybirds, for example), and also won't harm your pets (as long as they don't ingest it directly).

Purchase a neem oil product that is specifically for houseplant use and dilute with water in a spray bottle according to the instructions. Spritz the surface and underside of the leaves and repeat weekly until all evidence of the infestation has vanished.

KIT AND KABOODLE

While most houseplants and indoor-friendly edibles can be grown with minimal kit, there are a few things that will make your life easier. Here's the lowdown, from the essentials to the 'ohhh-that's-a-bit-fancy' investment items.

WATERING CAN

Whichever houseplants you opt for, they will need watering at some point. A small watering can with a long, narrow spout can be useful for getting under the leaves to deliver the water directly to the roots and soil, and also for controlling the amount of water you're administering. Some plants, such as cacti and succulents, don't cope well with tap water and need rainwater to look their best, so leaving your watering can outside when it rains, then bringing it inside to allow the water to reach room temperature works well.

SPRAY BOTTLE

If you're attempting to grow any plant that favours high humidity (see 'Five Plants for Your Bathroom', p.38), you'll need something to spritz it with. This can be any sort of spray bottle, from the standard plastic ones to lovely glass bulb misters that double up as ornaments and can often be picked up at charity shops. To keep costs down you can wash and reuse a spray bottle that previously contained hair products or cooking-oil spray – just be sure to remove all traces before use.

GLOVES

Strong, thick gloves will be useful for handling prickly cacti and for when you're re-potting plants to avoid getting soil under your fingernails. If you're growing any of the hotter chilli plants (see p.114), you'll also want to protect your skin when picking the fruits. However, specialist gardening gloves aren't essential – if you don't have any, thick rubber gloves will do.

TROWEL

Most garden centres have a plethora of trowels for sale, from the bog-standard stainless-steel ones to those with elaborate decorations, and even personalised with your name. While trowels are often sold as part of a houseplant kit, the truth is that for the minimal amount of digging you'll be doing as a houseplant parent, any old kitchen spoon will do.

HOUSEPLANT JOURNAL

Now, if you're taking houseplant growing very seriously, a journal can be useful for noting down when your plant babies need watering, feeding and pruning, and for keeping track of what was planted when. If you're not a journal person, setting reminders on your phone will work just as well.

MOISTURE METER

Many a healthy houseplant has been grown without the use of this gadget to monitor the soil's moisture levels, but these nifty little meters are relatively inexpensive and can be really helpful if you're growing a plant that's susceptible to root rot (such as chain of hearts – see p.52). Just pop it into the soil of the plant that you want to test and, within seconds, the colour-coded dial will tell you if it needs a drink or not. Simple.

SMART TRACKER

Now these are a serious piece of kit. These clever little gizmos sit in the plant's soil and link up with your smartphone via an app to give you real-time info on the health of your plant. Depending on the model, they'll monitor everything from soil moisture and pH levels to temperature, light and nutrients. They're definitely not essential, but they do make really good gifts for the tech-savvy plantista.

HUMIDITY MONITOR

If you're clueless about the humidity levels in your home, these inexpensive monitors can be a good way to learn. Whether you're just starting on your plant-parenting journey or are looking to invest in new members for your botanical family, a humidity monitor can save you from forking out on plants that just won't suit your environment. They can also be positioned near your plants all year round to check for fluctuations in humidity, and signal when it might be time to invest in a humidifier.

HUMIDIFIER

If you're a fan of tropical plants, such as hoyas or banana plants (see p.35), but aren't lucky enough to live in the tropics, a humidifier could be the way forward. These work by releasing a steady mist of warm or cool moisture into the air to raise the humidity levels. They are by no means essential – you can mist your plant manually or position a bowl of water near a radiator – but they are worth the investment if you're planning on growing a particularly fussy, humidity-loving plant in a bone-dry, centrally heated room.

ARTIFICIAL LIGHT

Some sort of artificial light will be needed if you're aiming to grow a light-loving plant in a low-light environment. They are also useful for getting seedlings going, particularly if you want to grow light-loving varieties, such as tomatoes, from seed (see p.123). All sorts of set-ups are available, from basic fluorescent tubes and LED lamps to super-fancy sun shelves that double up as coffee tables. The type you'll need will depend on the plant species, but with any artificial light source make sure you're not overdoing it and accidentally scorching your plants.

SELF-WATERING PLANTERS

These clever containers hold water in a reservoir below the plant and steadily deliver moisture to the plant's roots. They're a bonus for anyone who's away from home a lot, as you only need to top up the water occasionally, rather than having to water your plants weekly or fortnightly. Some also include a water-level indicator, so you'll know exactly when it's time to refill the reservoir.

10 PLANTS YOU CAN'T KILL

Here you will find ten of the hardiest house plants that can withstand moderate levels of neglect. Perfect for beginner plantistas and anyone who is away from home a fair bit. This isn't to say these plants will survive total abandonment – remember that all plants need light and water to survive as a minimum – but they won't keel over if you forget to water them once in a while or be fussy about which windowsill they sit on.

SPIDER PLANT

Great for scaring small children and arachnophobic grown-ups, the spider plant is so called due to its spidery offshoots, or spiderettes, which hang down from the mother plant. It's air-purifying and won't sulk if it gets a little chilly, making it a good option for cool, damp rooms. Allow the soil to partially dry out between waterings.

TIP
ESTABLISHED SPIDER PLANTS WILL GROW 'PLANTLETS', WHICH CAN BE POTTED UP TO CREATE BRAND NEW BABY PLANTS.

ZZ PLANT

Zamioculcas zamiifolia, or ZZ for short, is virtually indestructible and requires only very minimal attention to keep it in shape. This easy-going plant is a quick grower, likes low-light conditions and only needs occasional watering – if you met it in a bar, you'd definitely take its number. Water only when the soil is completely dry.

Looking to couple up with a low-maintenance plant partner? ZZ is the one for you.

Dracaena

Dracaena plants can grow to a whopping 3 m (10 ft) tall, so unless your ceilings are particularly high, you'll want to prune the cane (stem) every now and then to keep it under control. Not fans of bright light, dracaena are happiest positioned away from windows, and they thrive in moist, well-draining soils. Be sure to water before the soil dries out.

Pothos ➡

If you're looking for a houseplant that refuses to die no matter what you do (or don't do) to it, pothos is for you. Also known as devil's ivy, it lives up to its name and somehow manages to spread its bright green vines far and wide in even the most inhospitable conditions. It's a great starter plant for the first-time plant parent – perfect for cheering up student digs or a gloomy flat share. Water when you remember.

◀ PHILODENDRON

Adaptable philodendrons are the ultimate low-effort, high-reward houseplants. They require very minimal care and will do well in most environments, particularly if they can pop outdoors every now and then. Position in sunny spots with indirect sunlight and water when the top 2.5 cm (1 in) of soil feels dry.

PONYTAIL PALM TREE

This quirky palm, which is technically a succulent, has a tendency to look like it's seen a few too many late nights. But if the dishevelled look is your thing, it can work well in bright rooms (or in low light, where it can be placed outside in spring and summer) and likes to be left alone. The bulbous trunk stores water, meaning it won't complain if you're a little haphazard with the watering can. Water every three weeks.

English ivy

Most commonly seen climbing
the walls of country cottages
and hiding the doorways to
secret gardens, ivy also makes
an ideal and hard-to-destroy pot
plant. Plant it in a shallow pot
with good drainage, position in
a bright room and, other than
an occasional spritzing to keep
it clean, it won't need much
attention to thrive. Allow the soil
to dry out between waterings.

Boston fern

Space-loving and air-purifying Boston ferns can live for years in the right environment. They love cool humidity, so be sure to give them a light misting of water once a week, especially in winter when the heating is on. Unlike most of our easy-care plants, your Boston will need regular watering and a good soaking once a month. Your reward for a little extra maintenance is watching the vibrant green leaves slowly unfurl – plant poetry in motion.

JADE PLANT

Succulents are having a moment right now, and deservedly so. They're fantastically foolproof and easy-going jade is perhaps the most laid back of the bunch. With the ability to grow from a tiny cutting to the size of a small tree, all it needs to shine is careful watering, occasional fertilising and plenty of sun. Water when the topsoil is just dry to the touch.

TIP

CHECK YOUR JADE'S SOIL EVERY TWO TO THREE WEEKS AND ONLY WATER WHEN THE TOPSOIL IS DRY TO THE TOUCH.

SAGUARO CACTUS

This classic cactus is the ultimate buy-it-and-forget-about-it houseplant, thanks to its ability to retain water for long periods of time. Saguaros can grow to 12 m (40 ft) in their native Sonoran Desert, and live for an astonishing two centuries. While your indoor version is unlikely to reach such magnitude, place it in full sun and water fortnightly and you might find you're handing this prickly beauty down to your grandchildren someday.

Say salud to a saguaro from the Sonoran!

PLANT FIRST AID

Is your plant menagerie looking melancholic? If so, you need a crash course in plant first aid. Become a plant paramedic and you'll soon have the know-how to revive a critical cast-iron, resuscitate a flatlining fern and rejuvenate a jaded jade.

WHAT'S WRONG WITH MY PLANT?

Yellow leaves

Assessment:	**Assessment:**	**Assessment:**	**Assessment:**
is the soil saturated?	is the soil overly dry?	is the room cool or draughty?	are you feeding the plant regularly? If no...
If yes...	If yes...	If yes...	**Diagnosis:**
Diagnosis:	**Diagnosis:**	**Diagnosis:**	nutrient deficiency
overwatering	underwatering	too cold	**Treatment:**
Treatment:	**Treatment:**	**Treatment:**	invest in a good plant
step away from the watering can – you need to decrease the watering frequency and/or volume. Consider whether the pot has adequate drainage	get your plant on a regular watering schedule	move to a warmer room or consider an artificial heat source	fertiliser and follow the instructions on the packaging; alternatively, research homemade alternatives suitable for the plant type (see p.11)

Brown leaves

Assessment:
is the air particularly dry? If yes . . .
Diagnosis:
low humidity
Treatment:
mist the plant regularly with room-temperature water

Assessment:
is the plant in direct sunlight?
If yes . . .
Diagnosis:
sunburn
Treatment:
move out of direct sunlight and give the plant a good watering

Assessment:
are you feeding the plant more than is recommended? If yes . . .
Diagnosis:
overfeeding
Treatment:
reduce the use of fertiliser

Droopy leaves

Assessment:
are you watering the plant as advised? If no . . .
Diagnosis:
over- or underwatering
Treatment:
treat your plant to a regular watering routine

Assessment:
is the room too warm or sunny?
If yes . . .
Diagnosis:
heatstroke
Treatment:
move to a cooler room out of direct sunlight and water regularly

Assessment:
is the plant in a suitably sized pot?
If no . . .
Diagnosis:
root-bound
Treatment:
rehouse the plant in a larger pot so the roots can spread out and absorb water and nutrients (see p.11)

Spotty leaves

Assessment:
are the spots dark brown? If yes . . .
Diagnosis:
overwatering
Treatment:
reduce the watering frequency and/or volume

Assessment:
are the spots caused by dry patches?
If yes . . .
Diagnosis:
underwatering
Treatment:
water more regularly

Assessment:
do you live in a hard-water area?
If yes . . .
Diagnosis:
hard-water damage
Treatment:
use filtered (but unsoftened) water to mist your plants

Holey leaves

Assessment:
do you have pets? If yes . . .

Diagnosis:
nibbling

Treatment:
move the plant to a more protected area

Assessment:
can you see any insects on the leaves? If yes . . .

Diagnosis:
pest damage

Treatment:
treat with neem oil (see p.12)

Falling leaves

Assessment:
has your plant recently been moved? If yes . . .

Diagnosis:
environment change

Treatment:
your plant may be taking a while to settle into its
new home; wait a few days to see if the problem
subsides; if it doesn't, you'll need to
investigate further

Assessment:
can you see insects on the roots? If yes . . .

Diagnosis:
pest damage

Treatment:
treat with neem oil (see p.12)

No flowers

Assessment:
is the plant getting enough light?
If no . . .

Diagnosis:
light deprivation

Treatment:
move the plant to a sunnier spot
or consider an artificial-light source
(see p.15)

Assessment:
is the air particularly dry?
If yes . . .

Diagnosis:
low humidity

Treatment:
mist the plant regularly with
room-temperature water

Assessment:
is the pot too large for the plant? If yes . . .

Diagnosis:
unrestricted roots

Treatment:
re-home the plant in a smaller pot –
some will only flower if the roots
are restricted

Think outside the box (or drawer) to create insta-ready plant displays.

PLANT
MATCHMAKING

FINDING YOUR PERFECT PLANT PARTNER

One of the top reasons for houseplants failing to thrive is the wrong plant in the wrong location. All too often, inexperienced plant owners will place a low-humidity-loving plant in a bathroom, or a desert dweller in a dark corner, then wonder why the plant gets grumpy. Think of plants like people – city types may not be entirely happy thrust into rural seclusion, while country-loving folk probably won't be at home in the big city. Treat your plants with the same sensibility and your chances of success will dramatically increase.

Which plant is right for me?

Choosing the right plant can be a minefield. Will your personalities clash? A fussy plant might not be compatible with a laid-back owner. Will you enjoy each other's company? Buying a plant you hate the look of because it's easy to look after is unlikely to promote domestic harmony. And will you have enough in common? Trying to convert a low-light-loving plant to the joys of basking in the sun is only going to cause strife. Complete the quiz below to discover your soil mate, then read on for more ideas to suit your requirements and environment. There really is a plant out there for everyone.

YOUR PERSONAL PLANT MATCHMAKER

START HERE

Pets or kids at home?

NO — **YES**

Is your room sunny? — Is your room sunny?

Yes, it's bright and sunny. — Not really, it's a bit dark. — Yes, it's bright and sunny. — Not really, it's a bit dark.

What's your plant commitment status? — What's your plant commitment status? — What's your plant commitment status? — What's your plant commitment status?

Prefer to keep it casual. — Prefer to keep it casual. — Prefer to keep it casual. — Prefer to keep it casual.

Ready for a relationship. — Ready for a relationship. — Ready for a relationship. — Ready for a relationship.

Swiss cheese plant (see page 46). — Watermelon peperomia (see page 41). — Bromelaid (see page 35). — Gloxinia (see page 34).

Fiddle leaf fig (see page 49). — Lucky bamboo (see page 40). — Banana plant (see page 38). — Mosaic plant (see page 34).

Pets and plants aren't always a match made in heaven. Some pets love nothing more than nibbling on a leaf or chewing a stem, which can be fatal if the plant is toxic. No one quite knows why cats and dogs are so attracted to houseplants; theories include attempting to counteract a nutrition deficiency and fending off boredom. The best course of action is to keep all plants out of their reach, but by choosing any of the following you will ensure that disaster is averted if your furry friend simply can't resist.

MOSAIC PLANT

Also known as the rather ominous-sounding 'nerve plant', mosaics are, in fact, very pet friendly and thrive in low-light conditions. They can be difficult customers, as they need constant high humidity and aren't keen on direct sunlight, so perhaps not one for those who like a bung-it-anywhere houseplant; but if you're up for a bit of extra maintenance, they are well worth the effort. The mosaic's vividly coloured veins are more often white or green, but they can be found with striking pink or red veins – perfect for adding a splash of colour to a terrarium.

GLOXINIA

Along with African violets (see p.12), gloxinia tend to pop up in shops around Mother's Day and Valentine's Day. If you find yourself as a lucky recipient, you can rest assured that it won't harm your pets if they take a fancy to it. Gloxinia are relatively easy to care for and prefer moderate conditions with regular watering when they are in bloom. They're not long-lifers, though, and while they can flower more than once, their subsequent blooms tend to lack the attractiveness of the first flush.

BANANA PLANT

The domestic plants rarely bear edible bananas, so don't cancel your fruit-and-veg box delivery just yet, but they are one of the only large-leaved plants that won't get your pets in a pickle. Banana plants need plenty of light, lots of water and warm humidity to thrive, so do think carefully about your home environment before purchasing, but if you can meet its needs, the banana will reward you with rapid growth and enormous leaves. Perfect for filling an empty space and bringing a tropical feel to your home.

VENUS FLYTRAP

These, frankly, weird carnivorous plants are bad news for flies, but good news for pets – its 'jaws' aren't strong enough to harm animals or people if either unwittingly gets too close to the traps. You'll need to forget everything you already know about houseplant maintenance here, though – this is no ordinary plant. The Venus needs 12 hours of direct sunlight every day, acidic soil, tons of rainwater (not tap water) and to be fed with live insects (in addition to whatever it can catch). If you can deal with its rather exacting requirements, you'll have the added bonus of being able to watch your Venus devour its unsuspecting prey. Not for the faint-hearted.

BROMELIAD

Bromeliads are the lookers of the houseplant world and make great housemates for canines and felines. Originating from the rainforests, they are surprisingly adaptable and do very well in sunny rooms with high humidity (they're big fans of warm and steamy kitchens and bathrooms). They are available in a wonderful array of colours – choose one to match your decor – and aren't particularly high-maintenance, except for requiring a bit of careful pruning once the first flowers die. Keep yours moist with regular spritzing and you'll be treated to an exotic focal point.

Five plants for your bedroom

Any plant you invite into your sleeping area should evoke relaxation, so choose wisely (a Venus flytrap probably isn't the one for this room). Bringing greenery into your bedroom has the added advantage of helping to purify the air, boosting oxygen levels and literally making you feel more alive. Choose a plant with a relaxing aroma and you're well on your way to a peaceful slumber. Night night.

LAVENDER

The classic sleep-inducer, lavender has been used for centuries to calm busy minds and treat insomnia. With its attractive purple flowers and serene scent, it could very well be the perfect bedroom plant. The only drawback is that it won't last for ever indoors, so you'll need to move it outside once it's past its best, but it will usually tolerate a warm room for a few months. Be sure to choose a dwarf variety that is suitable for growing in pots and water sparingly.

VALERIAN

The root of the valerian plant forms the basis of many medications and herbal remedies designed to induce sleep, and for good reason – studies have shown that the herb can dramatically reduce the time taken to fall asleep. Allowing your valerian a good six hours of sunlight per day will result in blooms of pretty pink and white flowers, which are perfect for adding to a pre-bed bath for a relaxing soak. (Please don't eat your valerian plant – it won't taste very nice and valerian should only be ingested as an edible supplement.)

PEACE LILY

Confusingly, peace lilies aren't actually part of the lily family but are closely related to philodendrons (see p.21). Their ability to filter toxic gases such as carbon monoxide and formaldehyde from the air makes them ideal for bedrooms or any other room you spend a lot of time in (they'll look smart in your home office, too). Peace lilies like to be watered when they're looking a little limp and will thrive if you give them plenty of filtered sunlight and regular spritzings with a water spray; when well looked after they will bloom twice a year. Do avoid if you have cats or dogs, though, as they are toxic if ingested.

JASMINE

Wonderfully fragrant jasmine will fill your bedroom with its delicate perfume at night, creating a calming atmosphere as you drift off to dreamland. Be sure to choose a variety suitable for growing indoors to enjoy their bursts of white or pink flowers. Jasmine can tolerate cool temperatures and draughty windowsills – perfect if you like to keep your bedroom on the chilly side and sleep with the windows open – and a spell outside in the summer will help to keep their blooms blossoming.

CHAMOMILE

Invest in a chamomile plant and you'll have the added bonus of being able to brew the daisy-like flowers into a relaxing bedtime tea. The plants only need around four hours of sunlight each day, so are ideal for a spot where the sun is obscured for part of the day, although if growing from seed, longer periods of sunlight will be needed to encourage germination. Other than weekly waterings when the soil feels dry your chamomile won't need much attention, leaving you more time to enjoy your cuppa.

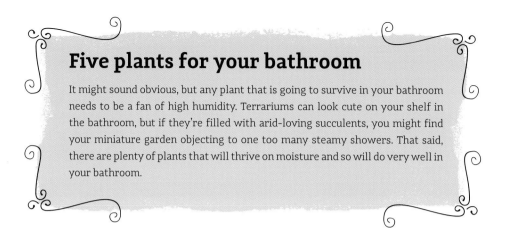

Five plants for your bathroom

It might sound obvious, but any plant that is going to survive in your bathroom needs to be a fan of high humidity. Terrariums can look cute on your shelf in the bathroom, but if they're filled with arid-loving succulents, you might find your miniature garden objecting to one too many steamy showers. That said, there are plenty of plants that will thrive on moisture and so will do very well in your bathroom.

BAMBOO

First and foremost, bamboo is not a plant to attempt to grow in a very small space or if you don't fancy re-potting every year. While a domestic bamboo plant won't grow at anything like the rate of its wild relations, it will send up new canes pretty much every year once established, meaning it can quickly outgrow its home. If it sounds like it might not be the plant for you, skip this one and save yourself the hassle. However, if you have a large space and aren't put off by annual re-homing, bamboo can bring a zen-like atmosphere to your bathroom and transport you to far-flung places while you soak. Be sure to choose a cultivar that won't burst out of its pot every few months and keep growth in check by cutting back emerging canes as needed.

ASPARAGUS FERN

The asparagus fern isn't actually a fern but is related to asparagus, which is confusing as it definitely looks more like a fern than an asparagus spear. Don't be tempted to see if it tastes similar, though – it's highly toxic and can also be prickly, so definitely one to keep out of reach of pets and small children. Park it on a high shelf in your bathroom in dappled shade and don't bother it too much, then you'll be rewarded with a cascade of feather-like branchlets.

MOTH ORCHIDS

The delicate beauty of an orchid is somewhat tainted by its reputation for being fantastically temperamental. Many of us will have been given one as a gift, only to have it promptly expire a few weeks later. While it may look stunning as a dining-table centrepiece, your orchid will be happiest in the bathroom, where it will thrive in the warm dampness. See pp.88–103 for more on these colourful beauties.

ALOE VERA

A dual-purpose plant is never a bad thing, and aloe vera is just that – its spiky leaves will look rather majestic on your bathroom windowsill, while the gooey insides can be used to soothe all manner of skin irritations. Simply remove a leaf, carefully slice away the green outer parts to reveal the clear 'gel' inside and apply this directly to the skin (see p.78 for more ideas). The shallow roots of aloe plants can be susceptible to rotting, so take care not to overwater yours, and choose a shallow rather than tall pot where possible.

AIR PLANT

These anomalies of the plant world absorb water and nutrients from the air, rather than soil, forgoing the need for pots. They will happily soak up the humidity in your bathroom while looking rather cool floating around in glass containers, as if suspended in mid-air, or artfully sprouting from a piece of driftwood on your windowsill. They are incredibly low-maintenance, but if your bathroom isn't being used for a while, you'll need to remember to spritz them with water every few days.

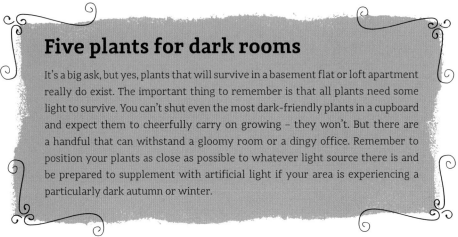

Five plants for dark rooms

It's a big ask, but yes, plants that will survive in a basement flat or loft apartment really do exist. The important thing to remember is that all plants need some light to survive. You can't shut even the most dark-friendly plants in a cupboard and expect them to cheerfully carry on growing – they won't. But there are a handful that can withstand a gloomy room or a dingy office. Remember to position your plants as close as possible to whatever light source there is and be prepared to supplement with artificial light if your area is experiencing a particularly dark autumn or winter.

LUCKY BAMBOO

Not to be confused with actual bamboo (see p.38), lucky bamboo is, in fact, a dracaena (see p.18) – so called because its stems look very similar to bamboo canes. It can live happily in almost full shade and will grow in soil or water. If growing in water, ensure the roots remain covered, topping up the water every seven to ten days, and don't be tempted to use tap water; your lucky bamboo won't like the chlorine. Living up to its name, lucky bamboo is often given as a gift to bring good fortune.

CHINESE EVERGREEN

These luscious plants have the most striking leaves in a variety of colours, from silver and green to hints of red. Their light requirements can vary, so when choosing a Chinese evergreen for a dark room be sure to select one that is dark green in colour as it won't need as much light as paler, silvery varieties. These are hardy houseplants that will reward you with full, lush growth for many years, but do avoid them if you have pets or small children who may be attracted to their toxic red berries.

BIRD'S-NEST FERN

Ferns are renowned for being unfussy and easy-going, but not all are suited to shade. Bird's-nest ferns can cope very well in low light and also won't object to moderate humidity, making them a great option for a damp basement flat. The new leaves emerging from the centre of the plant are said to resemble eggs in a nest (they don't, but the name is fun anyway). Once in situ, your bird's-nest will thank you for leaving it well alone, as handling can damage the delicate fronds.

HOYA

The waxy-leaved hoya is often grown outdoors as a climbing plant with unusual star- or heart-shaped flowers. Despite its native tropical habitat, it can do surprisingly well as a houseplant in a darkish spot, although it's less likely to flower. Pop it on a shelf or in a hanging basket to give its vines space to spread out and your hoya should be very happy in semi-shade.

WATERMELON PEPEROMIA

This small South American native gets its name from its striped leaves, which are said to resemble tiny watermelons. They are wonderfully unfussy and look smart on desks or grouped with other similarly sized plants. Other than perhaps not achieving such vibrant colours as when placed in brighter locations, watermelon peperomia will live very contentedly in the shade, provided the room isn't too cold and they are treated to the occasional spritzing with a water spray.

SENSATIONAL SHOWSTOPPERS

THE POSERS OF THE PLANT WORLD

Fancy yourself as a plantfluencer? You're in the right place. Here, you'll find ten Insta-worthy plants who like to be in the limelight. Shrinking violets they are not, from the aptly named pink princess philodendron to the finicky fiddle leaf fig: owning one of these prima donnas will instantly elevate your plantista status from novice to ninja. Take your pick from this selection of ten tremendous trailblazers, then learn how to showcase them to bring zing to your home.

ZEBRA PLANT

There's no denying it, zebra plants are stunning. Their glossy dark green leaves with contrasting silvery-white veins are striking as they are, but it's during the late summer months, when the unusual bracts appear, adding a shock of canary yellow, that the zebra really becomes a thing of beauty. But that beauty comes at a price: zebras require a lot of maintenance, faff and fuss to keep them alive. That said, if you're up for the challenge of recreating a Brazilian jungle in your living room, your reward will be foliage fit for a style blog.

WATER: ok, here goes. Saturate with lukewarm water every few weeks until the water runs out of the pot's drainage holes, then allow to drain. The aim is to fool your zebra into thinking it's in a tropical rainstorm.

LIGHT: think shaded leaf canopy. Direct sunlight will cause leaf burn, and too little light will prevent those stunning bracts from appearing.

TEMPERATURE AND HUMIDITY: won't cope below 15°C (60°F) or in rooms where the temperature fluctuates. Position well away from radiators and air-conditioning units. It needs 60 to 70 per cent humidity, so it's worth investing in a humidifier (see p.15).

GOOD TO KNOW: to encourage bracts to form, fertilise weekly in spring and summer. Prune the flowers as they wilt, always wearing gloves, as the sap released can be a skin irritant. Phew.

SWISS CHEESE PLANT

Of all the amusing plant names out there, Swiss cheese has to be one of the most random. It's said that the perforated leaves resemble the holes in cheeses made in Switzerland (they don't) and, confusingly, the term has been used in reference to several different plant species. Fortunately, the care needed for each of these holey-leaved wonders is more or less the same. All plants that go by the name are superbly easy-going, just needing a little support using canes as they grow, to prevent them sprawling.

WATER: water when the soil feels dry up to your knuckle and ensure your pot has large drainage holes.

LIGHT: very happy in indirect sunlight. These plants need light to develop their characteristic leaf perforations, so don't be tempted to place one in a dark corner.

TEMPERATURE AND HUMIDITY: thrives in warm, humid conditions. Place in bathrooms or kitchens or spritz the leaves regularly.

GOOD TO KNOW: probably best avoided if you have pets, as the leaves contain calcium oxalate, which is toxic if ingested.

Despite the name, this is not a plant to be nibbled, as the leaves can be highly toxic.

SNAKE PLANT

Snake plants pack a punch in more ways than one. Their eye-catching, spiky leaves have earned them the nickname mother-in-law's tongue (no comment), and their mottled green pattern is said to resemble a snake's skin. What neither title alludes to, however, is their friendliness as houseplants; they are fantastically low-maintenance, so are a good choice for the time-poor and forgetful, somehow managing to thrive in even the most inhospitable environments. A study by NASA found that snake plants filter toxins such as formaldehyde and benzene from the air, making them perfect for city apartments and bedrooms.

WATER: when the soil feels dry and only once a month in winter.

LIGHT: happy in low-light conditions; but to keep your snake sparkling, position it in steady, indirect sunlight.

TEMPERATURE AND HUMIDITY: not keen on draughts and exceptionally cold rooms; will do best at average room temperatures.

GOOD TO KNOW: choose a snake that has dark green leaves; in general, the darker the leaves, the healthier the plant.

FIDDLE LEAF FIG

Fiddle leaf figs are having a moment, and it's a big one. You can barely open a design blog or scroll your Instagram feed without coming across these tall rainforest-dwelling beauties. Confusingly, they don't bear edible fruit, and their high toxicity means they need to be kept well away from pets and children, but if no one in your home is partial to nibbling a stem or two, they make striking focal points. They have a bit of a reputation for being, well, *fiddly*, but with the right regime it's very possible to keep them looking lush.

WATER: water when the top 2.5 cm (1 in) of soil feels dry and reduce watering in winter. If in doubt, it's better to under- than overwater, as the roots are susceptible to rotting.

LIGHT: bright, indirect light. Prone to sun scorching (see p.71), so take care not to expose the leaves to direct sunlight.

TEMPERATURE AND HUMIDITY: 15–24°C (60–75°F). These plants are very fussy about temperature, and even small changes either way can upset their delicate constitutions. Position them well away from draughty windows and radiators and be prepared for a fair bit of sulking after a change of location. Try to recreate their tropical homeland by keeping the air moist with a bowl of water under a radiator or by regularly spritzing the leaves with a water spray.

GOOD TO KNOW: fertilisers made especially for fiddle leaf figs are available; however, a good high-nitrogen plant food will also do the trick.

POLKA DOT PLANT

These quirky little plants are perfect for adding a pop of colour. You'll most commonly find them with pink and green leaves, but if that's not your jam, you may be able get your hands on a polka dot with red, purple or white spotted leaves – as demand grows, so breeders are developing ever-more colourful cultivars. In their native Madagascar, polka dots can grow up to 90 cm (3 ft) tall; to keep your dainty domestic version contained you'll need to pinch back new growths and provide plenty of filtered sunlight to prevent it stretching up towards the light. Group together with plants in contrasting colours for maximum plantista kudos.

WATER: only when the top 2.5 cm (1 in) of soil feels dry, as they're very susceptible to root rot.

LIGHT: bright, indirect light. Too much direct sunlight will fade their vibrant colours; too little and your polka will become leggy.

TEMPERATURE AND HUMIDITY: spritz regularly to replicate that subtropical vibe or treat your polka to a humidity tray (see p.15).

GOOD TO KNOW: to keep your polka looking perky, pinch back (see Glossary, p.139) the top two leaves on each stem weekly.

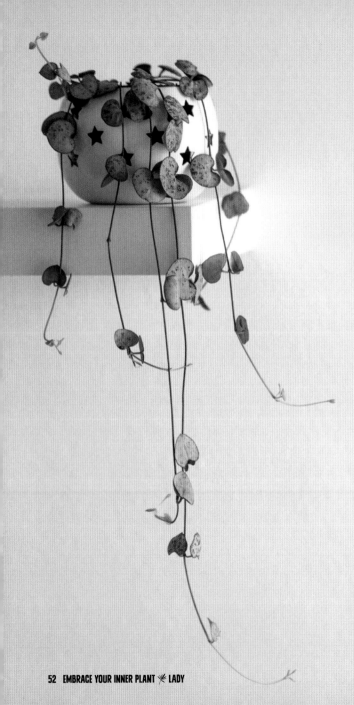

CHAIN OF HEARTS

Also known as rosary vines, these distinctive plants have unique long, trailing stems and cute heart-shaped leaves. The stems typically grow to around 90 cm (3 ft) – to fully appreciate their majesty, pop your chain of hearts into a hanging container or position on a high shelf, so the vines come tumbling down like Rapunzel's hair. Don't be tempted to lock them in a tower, though, as they need a little attention to stay looking their best.

WATER: this plant is very sensitive to overwatering, which will almost certainly kill it, so plant it in a container with good drainage and allow the soil to dry out completely between waterings. Alternatively, invest in a moisture meter (see p.15) to be absolutely sure when it needs a drink.

LIGHT: position in a sunny spot, as this plant likes lots of indirect bright light.

TEMPERATURE AND HUMIDITY: can handle the chillier end of room temperature and won't expire if your heating breaks down in winter.

GOOD TO KNOW: these are great air purifiers, so are a good choice for bedrooms or homes near busy roads.

PINK PRINCESS PHILODENDRON

The pink princess philodendron has caused quite a stir in the horticulture world, living up to its regal name. The bubble-gum pink leaves are due to a genetic mutation resulting in a lack of chlorophyll, and true pink princesses can only be grown from cuttings of existing plants. This fiddly process and a rise in demand have led some unscrupulous sellers to pass off artificially coloured pink Congo philodendrons as the real thing. Philodrama! If you're looking to buy one, make sure your intended has classic heart-shaped leaves that aren't entirely pink in colour.

WATER: only when the soil feels dry – pour water into the pot until it drains out of the bottom.

LIGHT: keep away from direct sunlight to maintain perky pinkness. Filtered light is best.

TEMPERATURE AND HUMIDITY: spritz with a water spray regularly or invest in a humidifier (see p.15).

GOOD TO KNOW: the leaves need at least some chlorophyll-containing green areas for the plant to be able to photosynthesise. If any leaves grow that are completely pink, cut them back to just above the leaf joint (where the leaf meets the stem).

RUBBER PLANT

This south Asian native can grow up to 60 m (200 ft) tall in its natural habitat, with leaves spanning 30 cm (12 in) in diameter. Remarkably, its super-strong roots have been trained to form bridges over lakes and rivers, and rubber was once made from the latex running through its veins (hence the name). While your domestic version is unlikely to form a bridge in your home, with the right care it will make a rather lovely houseplant. The beauty of the rubber plant is its large, glossy leaves, but they do have a tendency to turn yellow if the conditions aren't quite right. Keep an eye out for colour changes and refer to the advice on p.26 at the first sign of trouble.

WATER: rubber plants like their soil to be moist but not wet – don't allow it to dry out completely.

LIGHT: needs plenty of indirect light to keep the leaves glossy and vibrant. Plants with insufficient light have a tendency to become leggy.

TEMPERATURE AND HUMIDITY: spritz with a water spray every few days – those large leaves absorb a lot of moisture.

GOOD TO KNOW: keep the leaves clean by gently wiping them with a damp cloth (see p.12).

STRING-OF-PEARLS

So called due to its unusual spherical leaves that grow on trailing stems, this succulent is a great choice if you're after an unfussy showstopper that won't throw a strop if your plant parenting is sometimes a little haphazard. It looks stunning grown as a hanging plant, allowing the 'pearls' to roam free, but also works well in a wide, shallow pot with the stems circling together to cover the soil. However you display yours, you'll need to keep in mind that it'll most likely need to be re-potted every year or so. You can also easily propagate your pearls by popping a stem into a jug of water and potting when the roots are established.

WATER: string-of-pearl plants are drought-resistant, but very susceptible to root rot. Keep the soil just moist in summer, then only water when the leaves are beginning to flatten in cooler weather.

LIGHT: a sun worshipper, so it likes to be positioned in your brightest, sunniest room.

TEMPERATURE AND HUMIDITY: very happy in average-temperature rooms.

GOOD TO KNOW: plant in cactus soil and re-pot annually. After five years or so, your plant will have had enough of re-homing, so switch to propagating instead.

CAST-IRON PLANT

A great choice for first-time plant parents, cast-irons are virtually indestructible and can withstand all but the most serious levels of neglect. If you want to grow a photoshoot-worthy plant but aren't up for the faff of a fiddle leaf (see p.49), this one is for you. It also has very low light requirements, making it perfect for perking up dark nooks and crannies. If you're desperate for your cast-iron to produce its purple flowers, you could try moving it outside for a bit, although avoid very sunny days or position it in the shade as it can't cope with bright light.

WATER: not at all fussy about its watering regime, but less is definitely more. These plants are very drought tolerant – allow the soil to completely dry out between waterings.

LIGHT: loves shade, hates direct sunlight – position well away from south-facing windows to avoid leaf burn.

TEMPERATURE AND HUMIDITY: very happy at room temperature and won't sulk if you go away in winter and turn the heating off.

GOOD TO KNOW: Lennon's song cultivars have funky green and yellow striped leaves.

Cast-irons live up to their name as robust and hardy houseplants.

COOL
CACTI

UP CLOSE AND PERSONAL WITH THE PRICKLY WONDERS

Once the mainstay of Hollywood Westerns, desert-dwelling cacti have been in and out of fashion over the years. They are renowned for being an easy-care option for those who are yet to develop green fingers and have sustained a cult-like following since they were first grown as houseplants in the 1800s. These sometimes comedically shaped plants have held the fascination of horticultural enthusiasts the world over, even gracing Yves Saint Laurent's Jardin Majorelle in Marrakech. So, what exactly is a cactus? And are they really impossible to kill? Read on for an all-you-need-to-know guide to these prickly wonders.

The rise of the cactus

The name 'cactus' comes from the Greek word *kaktos*, literally meaning 'spiky plant'. Cacti are able to thrive in arid climates due to their unique ability to store water in their stems – a fully grown saguaro can store an impressive 900 litres (200 gallons). Native to desert and rainforest regions, such as parts of North America, Mexico and the Caribbean, cacti first landed in Europe in the 15th century, when Christopher Columbus brought one back as a gift for Queen Isabella of Spain. No one is quite sure what she made of her prickly present, but the gesture was instrumental in paving the way for cacti to become the superstar succulents they are today.

What Columbus couldn't have predicted was the rise of the cactus as a fashion statement. From catwalks to colleges, boardrooms to bedrooms, cactus prints are everywhere. *Brides* magazine even declared cactus wedding decor as a hot new trend in 2019, though it's perhaps best to avoid the spiky varieties in the bridal bouquet. Cactus-shaped handbags, mugs and lamps are all available, and for the true enthusiast there's even a car named the Cactus (so called by Citroën because much like a cactus is efficient with water, the car is efficient with fuel). Cactopia!

FACT OR FICTION?

THINK YOU KNOW YOUR PRICKLY PEAR FROM YOUR DINOSAUR BACK PLANT? CONFIDENT YOU COULD KEEP YOUR CACTUS CONTENT? TAKE THIS QUIZ TO FIND OUT HOW WELL YOU REALLY KNOW THEIR SPIKY STRUCTURES.

TRUE OR FALSE?

1. ALL CACTI ARE SUCCULENTS.

2. CACTI DON'T NEED WATER TO SURVIVE.

3. NOT ALL CACTI HAVE FLOWERS.

4. CACTI CAN LIVE FOR HUNDREDS OF YEARS.

5. ALL CACTI ARE INEDIBLE.

6. THE FRUIT OF PRICKLY PEARS ARE CALLED TUNAS.

7. ALL CACTI ARE PRICKLY.

8. SPIKASAURUS REX IS A TYPE OF CACTUS.

9. CACTI HAVE SPIKES TO HELP THEM STAY COOL.

10. MANY CACTI SPECIES ARE ENDANGERED.

ANSWERS

1. TRUE – ALL CACTI ARE SUCCULENTS, BUT NOT ALL SUCCULENTS ARE CACTI.
2. FALSE – LIKE ALL PLANTS, CACTI NEED WATER TO SURVIVE.
3. FALSE – ALL CACTI ARE CAPABLE OF FLOWERING.
4. TRUE – ALTHOUGH HOUSEBOUND CACTI HAVE A SHORTER LIFE EXPECTANCY.
5. FALSE – EDIBLE SPECIES ARE WIDELY USED IN MEXICAN DISHES.

6. TRUE – ALTHOUGH THEY BEAR NO RELATION TO TUNA FISH.
7. FALSE – SOME SPECIES HAVE SMOOTH SURFACES OR ARE COVERED IN FINE, WISPY HAIRS.
8. FALSE – ALTHOUGH DINOSAUR BACK PLANT IS A REAL NAME.
9. TRUE – THE SPIKES, OR SPINES, PROVIDE SHADE AND HELP TO PREVENT WATER LOSS.
10. TRUE – AROUND A THIRD OF CACTUS SPECIES ARE THREATENED BY EXTINCTION.

There are thought to be somewhere between 2,000 and 3,000 cactus species, ranging from the tiny *Blossfeldia*, measuring no more than 12 mm (½ in) in diameter, to the giant cardon, or elephant cactus, reaching a whopping 19.2 m (63 ft) tall. While your domestic cacti are likely to be of a more tabletop-friendly size, the principles of maintenance are broadly the same across species: a little water, a lot of sunlight and specialist cactus soil, designed to aid drainage and air circulation to keep your plant perky. So take your pick from the species on pp.64–47, put on your gardening gloves and prepare to get personal with these peculiar plants.

FINDING THE RIGHT CACTUS FOR YOU

Here you will find the lowdown on the most popular cacti to grow indoors. These are all suited to growing solo, or you might fancy grouping a few varieties in a container. However you choose to display your cactus, be sure to avoid closed or high-sided terrariums, as these won't provide the fresh air and low humidity your prickly friends need to thrive (see p.80).

◆ BARREL CACTUS

Definitely not one to keep within reach of pets and small children, as the barrel is covered with long, sharp spines – you'll certainly know about it if you get too close. Barrels can grow to a huge 3 m (10 ft) tall in their desert homes and have historically been used as a navigation device, as they grow tilted towards the southwest. Your houseplant variation will be a far more manageable size and will require lots of sunlight and little water to thrive (only water when the soil is completely dry).

Looking for low-maintenance, quirky houseplants? Look no further than this prickly selection.

OLD LADY ⬆

So called because its spherical stem is covered with fine white spines said to resemble an old lady's head, this unusual species is incredibly easy to grow and a good purchase for the first-time cactus carer. Old ladies belong to the aptly named powder-puff family, and happy plants will produce a halo of pretty pink or purple flowers resembling a crown on top of the 'head'.

ANGEL WINGS ➡

Also known as bunny ears, this cute cactus is a great choice if you want to avoid the prickly varieties; rather than spines, they are covered in thin hairs less likely to cause injury to small hands and furry friends. This Mexican native is a member of the prickly pear family and, given the right care and conditions, will bloom yellow flowers and grow edible red or purple fruit (said to be delicious when barbecued). Position yours in full sun, fertilise regularly and enjoy the fruits of your labour.

RAT TAIL ➡

An ugly duckling of the cactus world, the unfortunately named rat tail has its swan moment when its vibrant magenta flowers appear. While flowers are rare on domestic rat tails, they're not unheard of on mature cacti and this is a fast grower, so it's worth a go. You'll want to position it on a high shelf or in a hanging basket as the stems can trail down for almost a metre (3 ft).

◀ BISHOP'S CAP

The star-shaped bishop comes into its own during the flowering season (early spring and summer) when it develops glorious yellow blooms. To coax the bishop to bud, water sparingly and keep yours warm and sunny. Don't panic if you notice a white powdery coating – this is a defence mechanism to protect it from bright sunlight. Your bishop will thank you if you can add a little ground pumice to its soil to mimic its rocky Mexican homeland.

FAIRY CASTLE ▶

The wonderful fairy castle is a great hit with children – let their (and your own) imagination run wild with stories about who might live in its tall five-sided 'turrets'. Unfortunately, they rarely flower when grown indoors; if you've purchased one with flowers, chances are they're dried ones that have been glued on as a marketing ploy. But really, with a cactus this cute, who cares?

◀ CHRISTMAS CACTUS

This cheerful cactus is a great investment and with the right care it will burst into flower around Christmas time, year after year. Hailing from the rainforests of Brazil, it will appreciate filtered light and spells outdoors throughout the summer. However, in order to enjoy the blooms at Christmas, you'll need to go completely off-piste around six weeks before and move it to a cool, dark room (or cover it with a paper bag) for 12 to 14 hours a day. Once the first blooms appear, move it back to its usual spot and watch in wonder as the unique tubular flowers appear.

CARING FOR YOUR CACTUS

Now, if you choose to couple up with a cactus, you'll need to follow a few simple rules to maintain domestic bliss. It's not that cacti are particularly picky or demanding, but their care does differ slightly from that of most other houseplants. While you won't need to recreate a desert in your home, you will need to treat your cactus as the quirky creature it is in order for it to thrive.

Positioning

With the exception of rainforest dwellers (if you're unsure of your prickly friend's origins, check with the seller or online) who prefer dappled shade, most cacti will be happiest on your sunniest windowsill in a spot with good ventilation. They cope well with central heating but will thank you for a spell of cooler night temperatures in winter; if your cactus is positioned near a radiator, move it to a cooler spot in the evening then back to its regular sunlit location in the morning.

Watering

It's a myth that cacti hardly need to be watered; they do, but in a slightly different way to most other houseplants. If possible, water your cactus with rainwater at room temperature – succulents aren't keen on tap water, as the minerals can discolour the leaves. A good tip is to store your watering can outside to allow it to collect rainwater, then bring it into the same room as your cactus a few hours before watering.

In spring and summer your cactus will need watering weekly (or thereabouts) until water flows out of the pot's drainage holes. Aim for the soil to dry out slightly between waterings – it shouldn't be permanently moist – and add in a specialist cactus fertiliser once a month. In autumn and winter, you should only water sparingly when the soil is completely dry. Some desert dwellers may not need watering at all during the coldest months, as long as they are in coolish rooms.

Potting

Your cactus will probably have arrived in a snuggly fitting pot. Providing it has been planted in specialist soil, it will happily remain in the same pot until it shows signs of being root-bound (which is unlikely to be anytime soon, as most cactus varieties are slow growing). It might sound obvious but do protect your hands when handling your cactus; even the most harmless-looking spikes can become lodged in your fingers – and removing them isn't much fun. Thick gardening gloves or even oven gloves are good for preventing this.

Flowering

All cacti are capable of producing flowers, but the ease with which they will do so and the attractiveness of the flowers varies by species. If you would like to encourage your cactus to bloom, they key is to try to recreate its native environment. This doesn't mean turning your home into a Mexican desert; instead, it means mimicking the seasonal weather changes of your cactus's natural environment as closely as possible. Watering according to the seasons (see opposite) will trick your cactus into thinking it's experiencing a rainy season followed by a dry spell and will give it the best chance of flowering. Also, remember to clean your cacti regularly to allow for maximum light absorption. Use a soft paint- or make-up brush to gently remove dust from prickly plants, or a soft, damp cloth for smoother varieties.

Propagating

If your cactus is looking like it might have succumbed to root rot (see p.71), or you simply want a clone of it, it's really easy to create a whole new plant. This is best done in summer but can also work in cooler months providing the cutting has enough sunlight. Use a sharp knife to cut away a healthy, fully formed stem at its base and leave the cutting to dry out for a couple of days. Meanwhile, fill a small pot with a mixture of sand and specialist cactus soil and make a hole in it with your finger, around 2.5 cm (1 in) deep. Pop the cutting into the soil, pat the soil to firm and lightly water. Move to a warm, sunny spot and all being well, your cactus should take root in a few weeks.

HELP, I'VE KILLED MY CACTUS!

Ok – so despite your best intentions, you've discovered your cactus looking a little limp. Don't panic! In all but the most extreme cases it's usually possible to bring a cactus back to life with a little care and attention.

TIP
JUST A LITTLE CARE AND ATTENTION WILL KEEP YOUR CACTUS LOOKING COOL.

PROBLEM: brown or yellow patches
SOLUTION: these are usually a sign of sun scorching. This is particularly common if you've recently moved your cactus to a brighter spot or the weather has been unusually sunny. Try to filter out some of the direct sunlight or reposition your cactus until the sunny spell is over, and then prune away the scorched leaves.

PROBLEM: change in colour
SOLUTION: if your cactus is looking a little muted, or a previously brightly coloured variety has developed a greenish tinge, it is most likely due to light deprivation. Move it to a sunnier spot and watch it perk up.

PROBLEM: shrivelled or puckered leaves
SOLUTION: this is almost certainly caused by dehydration. Cacti are usually plump and plush due to their unique water storage system. If the cactus isn't receiving enough water, it will use its reserves and lose its plumpness. Refer to the watering advice on p.68 to bring it back to life.

PROBLEM: shrinking
SOLUTION: if your cactus appears to be shrinking or is looking a bit skinny, it could be etiolated. This fancy-sounding word basically means that its seasonal growing and resting periods have been disrupted and it's continued to grow through the winter. While you can't do anything about the weird shapes caused by etiolation, you can correct the problem by drastically reducing the amount of water the plant's receiving (or stop watering altogether) and lowering the temperature to below 10°C (50°F) to encourage the plant to go dormant until the spring growing season begins.

PROBLEM: weird growth patterns
SOLUTION: if your cactus seems to be having an unusual growth spurt, it may be that it's stretching itself towards a light source. Move the plant to a sunnier spot and be sure to rotate it regularly and normal service should resume.

PROBLEM: brown or black leaves or stems
SOLUTION: this is usually caused by overwatering. Carefully remove your cactus from the pot and check the roots for signs of discolouration. If the roots mostly look healthy, great – use a sharp knife to cut away the discoloured areas, re-pot the cactus into dry soil and water less frequently. However, if the roots are mostly black or brown, that's not so good. This usually means that the roots are rotting, and unfortunately signifies the end of the road for your cactus. If there are any healthy parts remaining, you could try taking a cutting (see p.69).

PROBLEM: change in texture
SOLUTION: if your cactus becomes soft or mushy, it may be receiving more water than it can retain, causing the cell structures to break down. It's vital to remedy this as quickly as possible to avoid root rot (see p.69). Ensure the pot's drainage holes aren't blocked, move it to a warm, dry spot and leave it to dry out.

SWEET SUCCULENTS

SLOW-GROWING STUNNERS

Confused about the difference between cacti and succulents? You're not alone. The classification has bewildered and befuddled plant aficionados since the Dutch East India Company shipped these otherworldly plants to Europe in the 17th century, prompting a quest for ever-more exotic species. The key thing to remember is that 'cactus' is a botanical classification within the succulent family, so while all cacti are succulents, not all succulents are cacti. Here, we're going to take a closer look at succulents that aren't cacti – for more on their prickly relations, see pp.60–71.

Easy-going succulents for beginners

As a general rule, succulents need similar care to their cactus cousins (see p.68): plenty of light, a little water and well-draining soil. Given the right environments, they're wonderfully low-maintenance and make a great choice for beginner plantistas. However, even the most experienced botanist has been caught out by a rather exacting plant. So, to get things started, take your pick from one of these chilled species and you'll be a succulent superstar in no time at all.

HENS AND CHICKS

Winning the award for the most randomly named succulent, hens and chicks are so called due to their ability to self-propagate; the main plant, the 'hen', produces clusters of smaller rosette-shaped 'chicks' in colours ranging from gold to blue. This alpine-dweller does well in window boxes and wide pots where it has access to around six hours of sunlight each day.

HORSE'S TEETH

This quirky succulent has cool rectangular leaves with translucent ends to aid photosynthesis. The fleshy green leaves grow in rows and are said to resemble teeth, hence the name. The plants usually only reach a few centimetres in height when grown indoors but their unusual shape makes up for the lack of stature.

TIGER JAWS

Searching for an eye-catching succulent that's really hard to kill? Look no further than the spiky tiger jaws. This South African native is used to the inhospitable clay soils of the subtropical desert, where it can be found nestled between rocks. Your domestic version requires little more than the usual care (see p.68) and a spell outside in the summer to keep those jaws sharp.

PADDLE PLANT

Also known as the yummy-sounding flapjack plant, the thick, rounded, grey-green leaves of the paddle will take on a rather lovely red hue when exposed to enough light; give the pot a quarter turn every week or so to ensure all the leaves are adequately sun-kissed. However, don't go too mad – as with all succulents, the leaves are prone to scorching and a brown tinge probably isn't the look you're going for.

GHOST PLANT

Who can resist a plant whose botanical subspecies name is *superbum*? Once you've finished sniggering, take a moment to admire the attractive grey–pink rosettes of this hardy succulent. The ghost has a tendency to become leggy if its light requirements aren't being met, so be sure to position yours near your sunniest window.

BURRO'S TAIL

The lush leaves and trailing stems of burro's tail (meaning 'donkey tail') make it a truly stunning and unusual houseplant. It's very unfussy, requiring little more than the usual high-light, low-water combo, and offers up maximum impact for minimal input. Position it in a hanging basket or on a high shelf to really appreciate its beauty.

SAY HELLO TO ALOE

If you only grow one succulent, make it an aloe vera. Their lush green leaves make a striking focal point, but their real beauty is on the inside. These spiky plants have been grown for their antibacterial gel for thousands of years and are one of the most widely used medicinal plants on the planet. This watery gel keeps their leaves plump and, well, *succulent* – and if you're very lucky, yours may flower once it's had a chance to mature. The magical elixir can be extracted from the leaves and applied directly to the skin to soothe burns and irritations (it's particularly effective if the cut leaf has been chilled in the fridge first) and is wonderful as an ingredient in homemade skin- and haircare products. (See opposite.)

PURIFYING ALOE AND COCONUT CLEANSER

To remove grime and make-up, mix together equal parts aloe-vera gel and softened coconut oil in the palm of your hand. Massage into damp skin for at least 20 seconds. Rinse a muslin cloth in tepid water and use to gently wipe away the day.

REFRESHING ALOE AND ROSEWATER TONER

For skin that sparkles, add 6 tablespoons of rosewater to a small bottle. Squeeze in around 2 tablespoons of aloe-vera gel (you may find a plastic funnel helpful). Screw on the lid and shake to combine. Apply to your skin using a cotton pad. Store in the fridge for up to six weeks.

CALMING ALOE AND HONEY FACE MASK

To soothe and reduce redness, mix a dollop of aloe gel (no need to be precise) with around half the amount of honey (manuka is particularly good, but whatever you have in the cupboard will work). Apply a thin layer to clean skin and relax for 10 minutes, then rinse.

PAMPERING ALOE AND COCONUT HAIR MASK

For luscious locks and a flake-free scalp, combine 3 teaspoons of aloe gel with 2 teaspoons of melted coconut oil. Apply to dry hair and scalp and leave for up to 30 minutes before washing your hair as usual. Say hello to soft and silky hair.

EXFOLIATING ALOE BODY SCRUB

To slough off dry skin cells and reveal the brightness beneath, measure out around half a cupful of granulated sugar and add half the amount of aloe gel. Add 1 tablespoon of lemon juice and mix well until combined. Apply to damp skin in a circular motion and rinse well.

SOOTHING ALOE AND VITAMIN E LIP BALM

For a perfect pout, melt together 1 tablespoon each of coconut oil, shea butter and beeswax in a heatproof bowl set over a pan of simmering water. Once melted remove from the heat and allow to cool. Add 1 tablespoon of aloe-vera gel and squeeze in the contents of a soft vitamin E capsule. Stir to combine, decant into clean lidded containers and apply to dry skin and lips as needed.

WARNING:

While it's pretty rare, some people are allergic to aloe vera – so if you're a newbie, it's always best to do a patch test before using any aloe-containing products. Simply rub a cut leaf on to an inconspicuous area of skin, such as the inside of your elbow, and if your skin still looks peachy 24 hours later, you're good to go.

TERRIFIC TERRARIUMS

Terrariums are back with a vengeance. Last popular in the 1970s, these miniature plant ecosystems have been revived and rebooted for a new generation. Succulents look super cool in terrariums – their small stature and interesting colour and shape combinations lending them perfectly to showcasing in glass. *But* these usually low-maintenance plants can be a nightmare to keep alive in these conditions and many a green-fingered millennial has been caught out by the terrarium's seeming ability to kill its contents overnight. Avoid the seven deadly sins overleaf and follow the tips to ensure your succulent micro garden retains its mojo.

FIVE SUCCULENTS TO TRY IN YOUR TERRARIUM

JADE PLANTS (SEE P.24)
TIGER JAWS (SEE P.76)
HENS AND CHICKS (SEE P.75)
ALOE VERA (SEE P.39)
PADDLE PLANT (SEE P.76)

SEVEN DEADLY SUCCULENT SINS

1 **Closed terrariums.** Entirely encasing your succulents in glass is a terrible idea. Remember that succulents need low moisture and good air flow to thrive. Put them in a closed terrarium and you're creating a humid environment with no fresh air, which is the exact opposite.

2 **No drainage.** Unless you've somehow managed to find a container with drainage holes, chances are your terrarium has a solid base, meaning there's nowhere for excess moisture to escape to. This can lead to root rot and is very bad news for your succulents.

3 **Intense heat.** Know that feeling when you get into a car on a scorching summer's day? That's what your glass-encased lovelies are having to deal with. Succulents do need plenty of light but position a terrarium in direct sunlight and you're literally cooking your plants alive.

4 **Crowding.** That beautifully curated selection of succulents might look cute and snug in their see-through home, but many terrarium enthusiasts tend to overlook the simple fact that plants grow. That snug fit becomes stifling when there's no room for the roots to spread out.

5 **Incompatibility.** Mixing up succulent species in a terrarium can make for a really stunning centrepiece, but you'll run into problems if the plants in your selection have different growth rates. The faster-growing plants will inevitably spread themselves taller and wider than the slower ones, hogging the light and depriving their smaller housemates of this life-giving resource.

6 **Humidity.** Terrariums are essentially a holiday camp for mould and fungi. Their high humidity and lack of air flow might not be ideal growing conditions for succulents, but microorganisms love them. Putting succulent-containing terrariums in bathrooms raises the humidity levels even further.

7 **Neglect.** Many first-time terrarium owners make the mistake of bunging their glassy wonder on a shelf and forgetting about it, only to discover a horrible brown mess weeks later. Succulents might be low-maintenance houseplants, but once they're in a terrarium it's a whole other ball game.

SEVEN STEPS TO TERRARIUM TRIUMPH

1 Choose an open container with low sides. To maximise air flow and prevent your succulents from overheating, you'll need a wide and shallow terrarium. This will also allow easy access to prune away unhealthy shoots and remove any fallen leaves.

2 Avoid overwatering. With nowhere for excess water to escape to, overwatering will very likely lead to root rot and almost certainly signify sudden death for your succulents. Water sparingly using a pipette and only when the soil is dry.

3 Use specialist soil. Whether you are creating a terrarium from scratch or buying one off the shelf, always make sure it contains specialist soil with little or no organic matter.

4 Avoid intense sunlight. Your succulents need to bask, not cook. Place your terrarium in filtered sunlight to avoid your plants experiencing the greenhouse effect.

5 Remove dead plants immediately. This may seem obvious, but all too often terrarium owners will hang on to a suffering succulent in the hope that it will come back to life. Remove dead plants as soon as you notice a problem to avoid whatever killed them affecting their housemates.

6 Prune overgrown plants. Succulents in terrariums have a tendency to become leggy as they compete for light. Prune back new shoots to keep yours in check and to avoid the overgrown plants plunging the smaller ones into shade.

7 Cheat! A great tip for creating the look and feel of a terrarium without the hassle is to place several succulents still in their pots into a pretty, low-sided glass container. To hide the pots, fill the container with soil, pebbles, decorative gravel or whatever takes your fancy (as the succulents are contained in their own soil it really doesn't matter what you use), then water and fertilise each plant according to its individual needs. Hey presto, you've created a succulent oasis!

CREATE A LIVING WORK OF ART

Growing walls and living artworks are having a moment in the plant world. As houses and apartments have become smaller, gardens have gone vertical to allow even the most space-deprived of us to show off our green fingers. Their small size and shallow root systems coupled with low water and high light requirements make succulents ideal for vertical planting. And creating a showstopping display isn't as tricky as it may seem. Take inspiration from these ideas and you'll soon have your very own living work of art.

Succulent wreath

Lush living wreaths look cool on front doors at Christmas and can also be styled as table centrepieces or hung on a wall at any time of year. They look complicated but actually couldn't be easier to create.

To get started, purchase a living-wreath base with a liner (available online) and select your succulents (small, colourful, rosette-shaped succulents such as hens and chicks work well). You'll then need to pack the liner with cactus soil, make cuts in it following the instructions and insert your chosen succulents. Your wreath will need to remain horizontal for a few weeks to allow the roots to establish themselves, but once everything feels secure it's ready for hanging. To avoid a waterfall, lay the wreath flat before watering and allow to dry before rehanging.

Box planter

For a really easy yet effective vertical wall display, choose a window box or other rectangular planter that doesn't weigh too much (if you're really handy, you could upcycle a wooden crate or repurpose a length of plastic guttering). Choose a selection of trailing succulents, such as burro's tail (see p.77), string of pearls (see p.57) or chain of hearts (see p.52), and pop these into the container still in their pots.

If you can see the top of the planter from where you intend to position the plant, you may want to fill it around the pots to disguise them – it doesn't really matter what you use as your plants won't come into direct contact with it, but make sure it doesn't add much weight. Then simply hang the planter on your wall using strong wall brackets. Hey presto, artwork in an instant.

Living mosaic

To create this stunning succulent artwork, you can either upcycle an old picture frame to make a planter by attaching the frame to a wooden box and covering the top with wire, or cheat and buy a ready-made succulent box frame (available online). Whichever route you go down, the principles for creating the artwork are the same. Fill the frame with specialist cactus soil to just beneath the wire, then make holes in the soil for your succulents to nestle into. Beginning with the larger plants, poke the stems into the soil so that the leaves are just above the wire – prepared cuttings from existing plants work particularly well (see p.69). Continue to fill the frame, packing the succulents as close together as the wire permits. Let the frame lie flat for two weeks out of direct sunlight and avoid watering. Then, providing all the plants are secure, your artwork is ready to hang. Always water when the frame is horizontal and allow the soil to dry before rehanging.

OPULENT
ORCHIDS

THE EXOTIC BEAUTIES

Graceful, otherworldly orchids have something of a cult following in the horticultural world. Their delicate flowers and statuesque stems make for a truly stunning display, and with a whopping 30,000 species there's most definitely a colour variety out there to suit your mood. However, they are notorious for being difficult to look after, seemingly throwing a strop the minute they cross the threshold into your home, and all too often that first flush of loveliness fades to a greying mess. The problem is that their rather exacting and sometimes contradictory needs are often overlooked, and these aren't plants to mess with – one false move and they're toast. So, read on to learn how to care for these exotic beauties and banish orchid woes for ever.

Get to know your orchid

The first step on your journey to orchid opulence is
to identify which species your plant belongs to. If
yours is newly arrived and still has its shop label,
be sure to make a note of the species name before
discarding the packaging. You won't need to pay
much attention to this initially, but it will be useful
info when you're trying to encourage your orchid
to rebloom (see p.102). If your orchid has been with
you for a while or doesn't have a label, you'll need to
play detective to determine its species. While there
is an astounding number of orchid hybrids – close
to 100,000 – the vast majority sold as houseplants
fall into one of two categories: *Phalaenopsis*, also
called moth orchids and *Dendrobium*, known more
commonly as cane orchids. Here, we'll also take a
look at the slightly more unusual varieties found in
garden centres and online retailers.

Phalaenopsis
(moth orchids)

What we might think of as classic orchids, plants in this family have elegant stalks topped with multiple delicate white, purple or pink flowers, with large, dark green waxy leaves. They are the most popular orchids all over the world, and if your plant was purchased at a garden centre or supermarket, it's very likely that it's a *Phalaenopsis*.

Dendrobium ➧
(cane orchids)

Dendrobiums have thick canes with thin leaves growing along their lengths and are becoming more and more popular as houseplants. They have smaller flowers than the *Phalaenopsis* family, growing in abundant clusters, and are typically white or purple. With the right care, they will bloom several times a year.

Support the stem with a cane to avoid orchid droop.

Cymbidium
(boat orchids)

These spiky-leaved orchids have small flowers in an astonishing array of colours and patterns, from bright pink to lime green and tiger stripes to leopard spots. What they lack in flower size they make up for in their spray of tall, prominent leaves that seem to emerge from the base like fireworks.

Vanda

Vandas are true epiphytes, meaning that their roots absorb moisture and nutrients from the air rather than soil. They are usually sold in glass jars or vases, or positioned on hanging stands, so are pretty easy to differentiate from their terrestrial cousins. If you're the proud owner of a *Vanda*, you'll need to follow the specific care guidelines on p.100.

Zygopetalum

The waxy purple and green flowers of the *Zygopetalum* family smell wonderful from autumn to spring, emitting a much-needed cheerful fragrance throughout the gloomy days of winter. The unusually slim petals, often patterned with black spots and stripes, make for a really striking table decoration.

Oncidium (dancing lady) ➤

Most *Oncidium* orchids are epiphytic and grow on the surface of other plants in the wild, absorbing moisture and nutrients from the air, but your domestic version may have arrived potted in specialist orchid compost. The bright flowers are said to resemble Latin American dancers and some varieties have the scent of cocoa.

TIP
TO KEEP YOUR PAPHIOPEDILUM
LOOKING PERKY, AVOID
OVERHEATING IT.

◀ *Paphiopedilum*
(slipper orchid)

The intricate fan-shaped flowers of the
Paphiopedilum family have earned these orchids
a bit of a fan base. These distinctive plants are prized
by orchid collectors, and if you've found yourself
with one in your possession, you can look forward
to enjoying their extraordinary blooms for
many months.

Miltoniopsis
(pansy orchid)

The bright, joyful blooms of *Miltoniopsis* orchids can
grow to an astonishing 10 cm (4 in) in diameter. Your
indoor version is likely to have more modestly sized
flowers, while still bringing a happy vibe to your
home. The flowers are said to look like faces, and
while this may be a matter of opinion, they do have
a cheerful pansy-like appearance.

ORCHID CARE 101

It's not rocket science, but to be a successful orchid owner you'll need to grasp some basic principles that differ slightly from other plant-care guidelines. A crucial point to get your head around is that the vast majority of orchids sold as houseplants would naturally grow attached to surfaces, rather than in soil. Epiphytic orchids grow on plants or trees, absorbing moisture from the air and nutrients from organic debris, while lithophytes burrow their roots down into the cracks of the rocks they inhabit in search of rainwater and moss. This means that an orchid's roots are used to being exposed to the air, and not the restricted environment of the plastic pots they are usually sold in. But with considered care, it is perfectly possible to give your potted orchid everything it needs to survive and thrive without the hassle of trying to graft it to a tree.

THE LESSER-POTTED ORCHID

If you're the proud owner of an orchid that arrived minus a pot, such as a *Vanda* (see p.95), you'll need to mist rather than water the roots to add humidity. A twice-weekly spritz with a water spray should suffice.

Where to position

Most orchids are native to the tropics, where they enjoy warm days and cool nights. While recreating a tropical oasis in your living room may be a step too far, there are a few things you can do to help your orchid feel at home:

- Don't position orchids near draughty doors or windows; they are not fans of being chilly.
- Do allow your orchid lots of filtered sunlight; direct sunlight will damage its leaves.
- Don't place your orchid on a shelf or windowsill above a radiator: it won't cope with the heat.
- Do cool things down at night; you might need to move your orchid to a cooler room in the evening, then back to its warmer daytime spot in the morning.

How to feed

Orchids only require very occasional dosing with a specialist orchid food, around every third or fourth watering in the warmer months and not at all in winter. You can buy slow-release drip feeds which are inverted and inserted into the pot. While these might be a good option for those who are a little forgetful, they're not really necessary, as adding a regular feed when watering does the same job (available from garden centres – use according to the instructions on the packaging).

When to water

In short: not as often as you might think, and even less in winter. Ideally, orchids would prefer to grow in high-humidity environments, where they can absorb moisture from the air. Most centrally heated homes have low humidity, making this impossible, so you'll need to provide your orchid with water in a way that won't cause the roots to rot.

The best way to go about this is to start by watering every two weeks and keep an eye on your orchid to see what the roots are up to. Remove the plastic pot containing the roots from the outer pot. Pour tepid rainwater (leave your watering can outside to collect rainwater and bring it inside to reach room temperature a few hours before you plan on using it) into the pot a little at a time until it runs out of the drainage holes. Allow to drain thoroughly before returning to the outer pot – any liquid remaining will promote root rot. In winter you'll need to reduce watering to once a month or stop completely if it's looking happy.

Check the roots weekly to see if your watering is up to standard:

- Green roots = your orchid is happy; keep up the good work.
- Brown roots = your orchid is drowning; reduce the frequency and quantity.
- Grey/white roots = your orchid is parched; up your watering game.

ARE YOU ORCHIDDING ME?

Aside from root rot, one of the most common reasons for owners giving up on their orchids is their failure to reflower after the initial showroom bloom has faded. Newsflash: your orchid dropping all of its flowers does not mean it is dead! Literally thousands of orchids are relegated to compost heaps every year because we mistake their dormant period for death. Most orchids only flower once a year and while it can be frustrating to see your once-lavish orchid reduced to little more than a couple of leaves and a stalk, with patience and the right care you can restore its splendour.

Bring back the bloom

Let's face it, no one buys an orchid for its foliage, so your orchid will almost certainly have arrived in full bloom. Most orchids will flower for up to ten weeks, so depending on how far into the growing season your orchid is, you've realistically only got a couple of months to enjoy its first flush. Once the flowers die, don't panic and definitely don't assume that your orchid is past its best. Follow these steps to ensure your orchid bounces back in all its blooming glory.

1 Cut away the stalk or flower stems. If your orchid has thin stalks, such as the ever-popular *Phalaenopsis* (see p.92), cut the stalk at the base once the last of the flowers have fallen off. This will allow your plant to put its energy into nurturing its roots and leaves and encourage a fresh stalk to grow. If your orchid is a *Dendrobium* (see p.92), or belongs to another species with thick canes, trim the flower stems away from the cane but leave the canes well alone as they store precious energy the plant will need to develop new flower buds.

2 Check the roots. Carefully remove the plant from its pot, shake off the potting medium (usually bark and moss), and cut away any decaying roots. You won't need to re-pot your orchid for a couple of years, so if this was its first bloom, you can return it to the existing pot as long as it's clean and undamaged. Add bark or a specialist orchid potting mix.

3 Find your orchid a home. Move your orchid to a position where the temperature drops at night. This could be a room that isn't centrally heated, or on a windowsill that cools when the sun goes down and heats up again at sunrise.

4 Water sparingly. Now that your orchid is entering its dormant phase its water requirements will be different from the flowering period; by how much will depend on the size of the plant. Continue to check the roots weekly and follow the guide on p.101.

Once the first fresh buds appear you can return your orchid to its flowering-period regime on p.101.

EAT WHAT YOU SOW

HOMEGROWN HERBS, CHILLIES AND OTHER EDIBLE DELIGHTS

Nothing on earth will make you feel more like a kitchen ninja than super-charging your smoothies or adding punch to your pudding with some good, honest homegrown produce from your very own kitchen garden. *But I don't have an outdoor space*, I hear you cry. Never fear – you too can jump on the grow-your-own train without an allotment, greenhouse or muddy wellies in sight. All you need to grow these tasty edibles is a sunny windowsill, a pinch of patience and a dash of organisation. So, prepare to amaze your dinner guests with homegrown herbs, badass chillies and the prettiest edible flowers.

Heavenly herbs

Culinary herbs are a great starting point for the newbie indoor gardener. Not only will growing your own cut down on the single-use plastic packaging most shop-bought herbs arrive in, you'll also have an almost endless supply on hand for whatever kitchen creations take your fancy. You only need minimal space to turn your kitchen windowsill into an edible garden – a window box is ideal, but most herbs will happily grow in whatever container you have available. And you can grow most of these flavour-packed kitchen staples from seed or purchase ready-sprouted plants. Happy herbing!

BASIL

One of the easiest herbs to grow, a well-looked-after basil plant will produce an abundance of vibrant green leaves. It's a fast grower, too, and can be ready to harvest in as little as six weeks when grown from seed. There are a whopping 60-ish varieties available, including Thai basil, lemon basil and Greek basil, but the one you're most likely to grow at home is Genovese. While there are subtle variations in taste between the different types, the care advice is the same for all.

Do

Position your basil plants where they can enjoy plenty of sunshine – they need around six hours a day.

Prevent your plants from going to seed (see Glossary, p.139) for as long as possible by pinching back the top leaves regularly.

Don't

Expect your supermarket-bought basil plant to last without re-potting. The plastic pot you buy will very likely contain several plants, and you'll need to carefully separate out the stems and re-house the individual plants in slightly larger pots to allow them space to spread out.

Uses

Homemade pesto, pizza toppings, salads, pasta dishes.

TIP

REGULAR HARVESTING WILL ENCOURAGE BASIL PLANTS TO BECOME FULL AND BUSHY. IF YOU'RE NOT USING THE LEAVES STRAIGHT AWAY, THEY CAN BE WASHED AND FROZEN (EITHER WHOLE OR CHOPPED), THEN ADDED TO DISHES STRAIGHT FROM THE FREEZER.

ROSEMARY

A fragrant rosemary plant is a joy to have in the kitchen; there's something about the scent that's both uplifting and calming at the same time. As well as adding flavour to a variety of dishes – from your Sunday roast to Parmesan biscuits – its natural antibacterial properties make it a popular addition to homemade deodorants and household cleaners.

Do

Try to recreate rosemary's Mediterranean homeland by providing full sunlight for as many hours of the day as possible.

Plant in cactus soil or mix regular potting soil with sand to aid drainage.

Don't

Overwater – waterlogged soil is the enemy of a healthy rosemary plant. Water when the topsoil feels dry to the touch.

Place in high-humidity environments, such as near a stove or steaming kettle; they prefer a dry spot with good air circulation.

Uses

Flavoured oils, roast potatoes, marinade for lamb, cocktails.

TIP

YOUR POTTED PLANT WILL LOVE A SPELL OUTDOORS IN THE SUNSHINE DURING THE SUMMER. HOWEVER, BEFORE BRINGING IT BACK INSIDE WHEN THE WEATHER COOLS DOWN, YOU'LL NEED TO PUT IT ON A SUNSHINE DIET TO PREVENT IT GOING INTO SHOCK. TRY MOVING IT INTO THE SHADE FOR A FEW HOURS EACH DAY, GRADUALLY REDUCING ITS SUNLIGHT HOURS UNTIL IT'S TIME TO RELOCATE.

CORIANDER (CILANTRO)

Homegrown coriander plants not only produce wonderfully aromatic leaves and stems, perfect for adding to curries and Thai dishes, but also offer up their seeds, which can be dried and added to your spice collection. Coriander plants aren't easily adaptable, so if you intend to keep your plant indoors all year, you'll be better off planting from seed than trying to encourage a shop-bought plant to thrive on your kitchen windowsill.

Do

Keep the soil moist – your plant won't thank you if the soil dries out – but not soaked.

Pick the leaves from the bottom of the plant first, as removing the top ones can weaken the plant.

Don't

Let it get too hot. Anything over 23°C (75°F) will tell your plant that it's time to flower, signalling an end to its usefulness in the kitchen.

Allow the plant to bolt (see p.138) by exposing it to too much sunlight.

Uses

Carrot and coriander soup, coriander chutney, Thai green curry, quesadillas.

MINT

When grown outdoors militant mint plants will do their utmost to colonise their neighbours, spreading themselves far and wide before you have a chance to brew your first mint tea. As indoor container plants they're less aggressive but do have a tendency to lean over and attempt to cover the surface they're on. Give yours plenty of room and watch out for wandering stems.

Do

Position away from direct sunlight. Mint is one of the few culinary herbs that prefers a shady spot.

Water in the morning when the topsoil feels dry to help your plant cope with any hike in temperature as the sun rises.

Don't

Allow any furry flatmates to nibble your mint plant. The essential oils it contains can be toxic if consumed in high quantities.

Pick more than a third of the leaves at any one time. This will weaken the plant and potentially stop it growing.

Uses

Mint tea, mojitos, mint sauce, tabbouleh.

TIP

MINT CAN BE SUCCESSFULLY GROWN IN WATER. SIMPLY PLACE A CUTTING FROM A HEALTHY, ESTABLISHED PLANT INTO A JAR OR BOTTLE OF WATER AND POSITION IN INDIRECT SUNLIGHT.

PARSLEY

It was once considered the height of sophistication to add a sprig of parsley to a dish before serving in a fancy restaurant. But this herb has far more to offer than merely being used as a garnish, and cooks the world over swear by its fresh flavour and natural affinity with seafood. It's also pretty easy to grow from seed, making it a perfect starting point for the first-time herbista.

Do

Stratify the seeds (see p.139) before planting by chilling them in the fridge, then soaking in warm water to speed up the germination process.

Turn the container every few days to stop your plant from leaning towards the sun.

Don't

Expect your newly planted seeds to spring into action immediately. Be patient and you should see signs of life at around three or four weeks.

Just pick the leaves. Parsley copes best when whole stems are removed from the base of the plant.

Uses

Chimichurri, salad dressing, parsley sauce, kedgeree.

OREGANO

The intense flavour of the fresh leaves from a healthy oregano plant bear little resemblance to the rather sad, dried-out supermarket version of this herb sold in jars. Once you've tasted the homegrown version, there's no going back. It's said to have antioxidant and anti-inflammatory properties too and has been used for centuries to treat common ailments such as indigestion and arthritis.

Do

Position in full sun – your plant needs maximum sunlight to develop its pungent flavour profile.

Cut whole stems for use, rather than a few leaves at a time, to encourage new shoots to grow in their place.

Don't

Confuse oregano with marjoram. While the two are related, marjoram has a more subtle, sweeter flavour and may not give the same results when used in cooking.

Uses

Greek salad, chilli, moussaka, Bolognese.

TIP

THIS IS A PROLIFIC GROWER AND EVEN A SINGLE PLANT IS LIKELY TO PRODUCE MORE LEAVES THAN YOU'LL BE ABLE TO USE. TO PRESERVE THE LEAVES FOR FUTURE USE, FREEZE IN ICE-CUBE TRAYS IMMEDIATELY AFTER PICKING AND USE DIRECTLY FROM THE FREEZER.

CHEERFUL CHILLIES

Whether you're a fan of blow-your-head-off Scotch bonnets, or more into the mellow hit of heat from a jalapeño, there's a chilli variety out there for you. And what's more, chilli plants are relatively easy to grow at home, giving you the advantage of being able to use the fruit straight from the plant when they're literally bursting with flavour. Chilli plants make cool gifts for the hot-food lovers in your life, so plant a few varieties in personalised pots (see p.134) for maximum present-giving points.

Hot and healthy

Not only are homegrown chillies the ultimate way to fire up your food, they also deliver on the health front too. Chillies contain a whopping seven times more vitamin C than oranges, and are also packed with vitamins A and E. They are rich in beta-carotene, folic acid and potassium, and loaded with capsaicin, which has been used for centuries to release endorphins and act as a natural painkiller (ironic, given the pain that can be inflicted by biting into a super-hot variety). Regularly eating moderately spicy food has been linked to a decreased occurrence of heart disease, too.

How hot can you go?

The most important decision you'll make when embarking on your chilli challenge is which variety to grow. There's little point in seeking out a Trinidad scorpion if the very thought of it makes your eyes water, or in cultivating a pimientos de Padrón if it'll never provide the punch you're after. Helpfully, scientist and chilli champion Wilbur Scoville developed a method to measure and categorise the heat sensation of different varieties by measuring their concentration of capsaicin – the chemical responsible for making them hot. So, take a look at the chart here and choose a chilli to suit your palate.

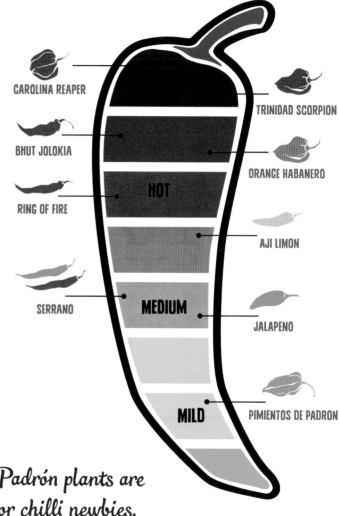

CAROLINA REAPER

TRINIDAD SCORPION

BHUT JOLOKIA

ORANGE HABANERO

RING OF FIRE

HOT

AJI LIMON

SERRANO

MEDIUM

JALAPENO

MILD

PIMIENTOS DE PADRON

Pimientos de Padrón plants are a good option for chilli newbies.

TEN CHILLI VARIETIES - FROM EXPLOSIVE TO EASY-GOING

CAROLINA REAPER

This cross between the ghost pepper and red habanero was bred for heat, and my goodness, does it deliver. It was listed as the world's hottest chilli in the 2013 Guinness World Records, taking the title from the Trinidad scorpion. If you're brave enough to give this a go, use extremely sparingly and always wear gloves and eye protection when handling the fruit.

HEAT RATING:)))))))))))

TRINIDAD SCORPION

An ominously named chilli plant, this one originates from Moruga in Trinidad and Tobago where the vivid red and yellow fruits grow in abundance on tall, majestic plants. Your domestic plant could reach up to 70 cm (27.5 in) in height and provide enough chilli heat to kick you into next week.

HEAT RATING:)))))))))

GHOST PEPPER

The ghost pepper, or *bhut jolokia* as it's also known, was cultivated in northeast India where the army use the fruits to make non-lethal weapons. These chilli grenades are designed to incapacitate the target by causing extreme irritation. If that doesn't put you off, expect your homegrown plants to produce 5 cm (2 in) chillies packed with intense heat.

HEAT RATING: 🌶🌶🌶🌶🌶🌶🌶🌶

SCOTCH BONNET

Contrary to its rather genteel-sounding name, the Scotch bonnet is a fiery force to be reckoned with. The fruits are said to resemble the traditional Scottish tam o' shanter hat (hence the name), but these perky chillies are more likely to be found growing in the Caribbean than the Scottish Highlands.

HEAT RATING: 🌶🌶🌶🌶🌶🌶🌶

ORANGE HABANERO

The bright orange fruits of this habanero variety have a unique smoky citrus flavour, making them a popular choice for sauces. If you only want to grow one type of chilli, and can handle the heat, this is a good option as it will impart a bit of flavour to your dishes, along with the usual warmth.

HEAT RATING:

RING OF FIRE

Don't be put off by the name – the cayenne-style fruits of this fast-growing plant are great all-purpose chillies to have on hand in the kitchen. They're particularly popular in Thai dishes but work well in pretty much anything you want to spice up. Pick the chillies when they are still green for a milder flavour or leave to ripen to a deep red for a more intense hit.

HEAT RATING:

AJI LIMON

The bright yellow fruits of this Peruvian native grow to around 8 cm (3 in) and will look pretty spectacular as part of your indoor kitchen garden. The plant has a tendency to lean over, so you'll either need to give it some support with a stake or two or position it on a high windowsill where it can lean all it likes.

HEAT RATING:

SERRANO

Originating from the *sierras*, the mountain regions of Mexico, serrano chillies are a classic addition to spicy salsa and hot guacamole. They taste like a slightly hotter jalapeño and are a good choice for anyone who likes a bit of heat without the eye-watering, mouth-burning sensation of chillies higher up the heat scale.

HEAT RATING:

JALAPEÑO

The classic jalapeño is probably the most widely used chilli in the world. Sliced on pizzas or pickled in jars, the green fruits are a familiar sight; but they can also be ripened to bright red and dried, smoked and sold as chipotle peppers. A versatile choice for the beginner chilli grower.

HEAT RATING:

PIMIENTOS DE PADRÓN

If you've ever eaten a fried chilli dish at a tapas bar, chances are you were eating pimientos de Padrón. These small green chillies are popular in Spanish cuisine and are usually picked and served while they are underripe, before their full heat intensity has had a chance to develop. Despite the low heat rating, they still pack a punch and can be left on the plant a little longer if you're after more of a kick.

HEAT RATING:

TOP TEN STEPS TO CHIRPY CHILLIES

1 Plant a few more seeds than you think you'll need. Not all will germinate, so more is more here.

2 Plant seeds in late winter in good-quality seed compost, around 5 mm (1/4 in) below the surface.

3 Move your newly planted seeds to the warmest place possible – next to a radiator is ideal.

4 Spritz the surface of the soil with a tepid water spray. Never use cold water.

5 Leave to propagate. Depending on the variety, you should see shoots in two to five weeks.

6 Once the seedlings have sprouted, your chilli plant will need light as well as heat, so move to a bright, sunny windowsill.

7 Continue to water sparingly when the soil feels dry, always using tepid water.

8 Support taller or drooping plants by carefully tying the stems to wooden stakes using string or twine.

9 Pick the chillies when they are firm, fat and waxy – exact timings will depend on the variety but remember that immature chillies generally have a milder flavour.

10 Use the chillies straight away or freeze or dry them (in the oven or using a dehydrator) for later use.

SUPER SALADS

Your indoor kitchen garden can really deliver when it comes to knocking up a sensational salad. A whole host of edible lovelies can be grown on your windowsill, but here we'll focus on those requiring the least fuss and fanfare. And don't forget to add your homegrown herbs and chillies, too, for an artisan feast fit for any foodie.

GROW A RAINBOW ON YOUR WINDOWSILL.

TOMATOES

To grow bright, juicy tomatoes indoors, you need to choose a variety suited to container growing and be sure to water carefully: too little and the plant will wilt and weaken, too much and your tomatoes will split and taste mushy. It's a good idea to buy tomato plants for your windowsill garden rather than attempting to grow from seed, as the hard work of trying to get them to propagate will have been done for you. Whichever variety you go for, your seedlings will need plenty of full sun and fortnightly doses of a specialist tomato fertiliser to keep them perky.

◄ SPRING ONIONS (SCALLIONS)

Ever noticed that shop-bought spring onions come with their roots still attached? Well, next time you're about to toss the ends into your food-waste bin, stop, and instead pop them into a jar of water (you'll need to retain all of the white part and a centimetre or so of the green part of the onion, as well as the roots). Change the water daily until the roots have grown to around 5 cm (2 in), then move the onions to a shallow container of potting compost. Keep the soil moist and watch your onions grow.

ROCKET (ARUGULA)

Unlike many of its edible garden neighbours, peppery rocket actually does very well in cooler temperatures, making it a good option if your kitchen is a bit on the Baltic side. It also loves a north-facing window, so it can even work if your growing space is a little sun-starved (although you may find the leaves turning yellow if its particularly deprived). A good trick is to sow seeds every two weeks during the spring and summer, to ensure a continuous supply.

MICROGREENS ➡

Anyone, and I mean anyone, can grow microgreens. They are the ultimate addition to an urban kitchen garden, needing only a tiny amount of space and a teeny bit of care. Microgreen seeds are available as individual varieties, such as beetroot, kale, broccoli and Swiss chard, or as seed mixes containing varieties with similar growth rates. All you need to do is fill a shallow bowl or dish, or even old yoghurt pots, with compost, sprinkle over the seeds, keep the soil moist using a water spray and cut your greens at soil level using scissors when they are a few centimetres tall (which can be in as little as a week). For a constant supply, keep sprinkling seeds over the compost every week or so.

EDIBLE FLOWERS

Nothing will elevate your salad from mundane to magnificent like adding a few edible flowers into the mix. A surprising number of flowers can be eaten, from roses and sunflowers to daisies and chrysanthemums, but by growing a batch especially for this purpose you can be sure you're not inadvertently mistaking a palatable variety for something a little less friendly. The easiest way to add a floral touch to your lunch is to plant a mix of seeds sold specifically for this purpose, then snip them when they look pretty.

A NOTE ON AVOCADOS

AS MUCH AS WE'D ALL LOVE TO USE HOMEGROWN PRODUCE FOR OUR AVO TOAST, UNLESS YOU'RE HAPPY TO WAIT A FEW YEARS FOR YOUR BRUNCH, YOU MIGHT NEED TO ACCEPT THAT THIS PROBABLY ISN'T GOING TO HAPPEN. WHILE IT'S PERFECTLY POSSIBLE TO GROW AVOCADO PLANTS INDOORS, BOTH FROM SEEDS AND AVOCADO STONES, THEY ARE UNLIKELY TO BEAR FRUIT FOR MANY YEARS, IF AT ALL. SORRY TO BURST YOUR AVOCADO-SHAPED BUBBLE . . .

Make your salad sing with a scattering of these homegrown pretty lovelies.

POT IT
LIKE IT'S HOT

GETTING CREATIVE WITH YOUR PLANT HOLDERS

Pots. They may not be the most exciting aspect of houseplant maintenance, but they sure are important. From the material to the size, to what you fill them with, the containers you choose as homes for your plant babies are crucial to their wellbeing and longevity. But what type should you go for? How often should you re-pot? And does the type of soil really matter? Read on to demystify the potting process and you'll soon be potting with the best of them.

When, what, how?

Chances are your houseplants will have arrived at their new home already in pots (unless you're growing from seed, in which case skip to 'What?'). In general, most houseplants need a re-pot every year or two, depending on their variety and growth rate. Your job is to check that the pot is the right size and re-pot as needed, then keep an eye on the plants for signs that it's time for new home.

WHEN?

Houseplants are pretty good at letting us know when they need a little more space. If possible, re-pot in the spring at the beginning of the growing cycle, but don't wait if your houseplant is displaying these indicators that it's in need of an upgrade:

- **Root-bound:** this literally means that the roots have run out of space and are having trouble absorbing the water and nutrients the plant needs to grow. To check if the root system is healthy, very gently remove the pot. If the roots are circling the base of the pot, are grouped together or have escaped through the pot's drainage holes, it's time to treat your plant to a new home.

- **Excessive thirst:** if your plant seems particularly thirsty and is wilting despite regular watering, it could be that the ratio of roots to soil has become too great, meaning that the roots aren't able to absorb water adequately.

- **Slow growth:** if your plant's growth rate seems unusually slow for the time of year (don't forget that many plants have a winter dormancy period), it may be that its root system needs more space to spread out.

- **Top heavy:** in general, the exposed parts of the plant (i.e. those above the soil line) shouldn't take up more than three times the pot space. If the balance has been tipped, you may find that your plant becomes top heavy and falls over easily.

WHAT?

There's no complicated science involved in choosing a pot. As a rule of thumb, you'll want a clean, undamaged container that's one or two sizes larger than the pot you're replacing (for most average-sized houseplants this will be 5–10 cm (2–4 in) larger in diameter than the previous pot). If you're growing from seed, the size of the pot will very much depend on the plant's root system and growth rate, so check with the seller or online.

And remember that your plant holder doesn't necessarily need to be a traditional circular pot – houseplants have been successfully grown in all manner of weird and wonderful containers (even decommissioned toilets!). The important thing is that any container you're using has adequate drainage. If you're going for an unconventional plant home or a conventional pot that doesn't have drainage holes, you'll need to consider a pot within a pot to allow excess moisture an escape route.

HOW?

Many a plantista has got their gardening gloves in a twist over the correct method for re-potting. The truth is that it's not at all complicated, but you will need to work very carefully to avoid damaging the roots. Follow these easy steps for successful plant relocation:

1. Remove the old pot. Hold your plant by the stem and tilt it on its side. If the pot can't be easily removed, you might need to give it a couple of taps on the rim. If the roots have escaped through the drainage holes and can't be coaxed away from the pot, you may need to cut a plastic pot away or take a hammer to a ceramic or terracotta pot.

2. Free the roots. Gently tease the roots with your fingers to encourage them to spread out. If the plant was badly root-bound in its previous home you may need to untangle them as best you can, or even trim them with scissors if they're particularly congested. Also, watch out for any decaying roots and cut away any areas that are black or look mouldy.

3. Shake off the old soil. Your plant will have been busy removing nutrients from its previous potting mix, so you'll want to treat it to some new nourishment. Try not to remove more than a quarter to a third of the soil and, if it's very firm, you may need to loosen it by gently running the roots under a tap (tepid water).

4. Fill the container with new soil. The type of soil to go for will depend on your plant type (see right), but the method is the same: hold your plant steady in the new pot so that the base of the stem, where the plant met the soil in its old pot, is around 2.5 cm (1 in)

below the rim; fill the pot with appropriate potting mix – avoid filling the soil above the base of the stem – and gently tap the pot to remove any air pockets.

5. Water and allow to rest. Give your plant a good drink according to its particular needs, then move it to a shady spot (even if it's a sun worshipper) and leave it to rest for a week or so, watering again if the top of the soil feels dry. Your plant needs a bit of calm after the storm to allow it to repair its roots and settle into its new abode.

A ROUGH GUIDE TO SOIL

The type of soil your houseplant or edible plant will be suited to entirely depends on its variety, its drainage needs and its native environment. You should always check the advice for your individual plant, but as a starting point, here's a very rough guide to the soil you'll find on sale in your local garden centre:

All-purpose potting mix:
this is your go-to soil, suitable for most houseplants without specific drainage needs.

Cacti and succulent mix:
contains grit and sand to aid drainage.

Orchid mix: a mixture of bark and clay, designed to aid air flow.

Compost for edibles: available in a plethora of varieties for everything from herbs to citrus fruits. You'll only need one type for your kitchen garden – choose a good all-purpose vegetable-growing mix to cover all bases.

PLANT POT MAKEOVERS

There's no two ways about it – plant pots can be pricey and a bit cumbersome to carry home if you're on foot or public transport. Finding one you like, that's the right size and within budget can be a brain ache. But there's really no need to splash out. Upcycling an old pot or customising a cheap plastic one is quick, easy and won't break the bank. Here's how.

Paint job

The most straightforward way to jazz up a pot is to paint it. You'll need:

- acrylic paints
- a large brush or sponge for the base coat
- small brushes, stencils or stamps with ink for the pattern
- paint sealer (not essential, but it will help your paint job to last.

Yard sales and thrift stores can be great for picking up cheap supplies for your plant pot projects.

1 Start by painting or sponging on a base coat of acrylic paint in your chosen colour (for maximum effect this should be lighter than the paints or ink you'll be using for the pattern) and leave it to dry thoroughly. You could also use a spray paint for speed.

2 While the paint is drying, practise your chosen design on a scrap of paper. Simple geometric shapes are very effective, as are stripes and spots. If you're not blessed on the artistic front, a stencil is a great way to go. Or, for a minimalist look, stamp the plant's name (particularly good for herbs) or a message for the recipient (if it's a gift) on to the pot.

3 Once your pot is dry, go wild and paint, stamp or stencil to your heart's content.

4 When you're happy with the design, leave the paint to dry and add sealer according to the instructions on the packaging. Hey presto, a customised pot is yours to behold.

Macramé pot hangers

Macramé may look complicated, but if you're no wizard in the craft department and don't want to fork out for a ready-made one, you can make a really attractive yet super-simple macramé hanger in minutes using coloured rope, thick wool or even strips of material. After all, macramé is basically just tying knots, so if you can tie a shoelace you can do this. Look online for a simple tutorial and get knotting.

Wrap it up

Wrapping rope, twine or thick wool in a spiral around your pot will not only hide what's lurking beneath, it looks pretty cool, too. No special skills needed here – just select colours to suit your scheme and invest in some strong glue (a glue gun is good for this, if you happen to have one). Starting at the top of the pot, glue the end of your rope, twine or wool in place then continue wrapping and gluing all the way down to the bottom of the pot, swapping colours or textures as you go, as the mood takes you.

The natural look

To bring the outside in, go foraging for decorative elements to attach to the outside of your pot. You could paint your pot first (see p.134) or leave it as it is. Shells, twigs and bark are effective, or you could also try dried flower petals. Once you have your materials, play around with designing a pattern on your work surface – it will be tricky and messy to reposition things once they're attached to your pot, so it's a good idea to come up with a design you're happy with before reaching for the adhesive. Once you've perfected your pattern, get gluing.

If in doubt, cheat

If the idea of painting, knotting or gluing your way to a fancy plant holder fills you with dread, or you simply don't have the time to mess about with designing your own creation, the answer is to cheat. Placing your unsightly plastic pot into another container instantly elevates it from cheap to chic. Brilliant options are hessian bags, which can be folded over for a slouchy look, or those cute canvas storage bags or trugs that can be picked up for a few pounds. You'll need to place a saucer in the base (to catch water) before adding your plant pot, but that's pretty much it. Elegance in an instant.

GLOSSARY

ANNUAL A plant that completes its life cycle in one growing season.

BLANCHED Parts of a plant, particularly the leaves, that have become faded in colour.

BOLTING When a plant flowers and goes to seed prematurely.

BRACT A type of modified leaf that grows below the plant's flowers.

BUD A new growth forming from the stem.

CACTI Succulent plants from the *Cactaceae* family.

CHLOROPHYLL Gives plants their green colour and has a role in photosynthesis.

COMPOST A potting medium containing organic matter to help plants grow.

CULTIVAR A plant that comes into existence through cultivation, rather than occurring naturally in the wild.

DAPPLED LIGHT Sunlight that is partially shaded.

DORMANCY The period when a plant's growth slows or stops, usually over winter.

ETIOLATION Prolonged or unusual growth of a plant due to a lack of daylight.

EPIPHYTE A plant that grows on other plants or surfaces, rather than in soil, usually absorbing water and nutrients from its surroundings.

GERMINATION The process of a seed sprouting, usually after a period of dormancy.

GOING/GONE TO SEED When a plant enters the flowering stage in preparation for seed production.

HERBACEOUS A plant with no woody stem above ground level.

HYBRID A new plant that is the result of a cross between two botanically distinct species.

IRRIGATE Water to help growth.

LEGGY Term used to describe a plant that has grown unevenly or unusually tall, often due to light deprivation or insufficient pruning.

LOW LIGHT Little or no direct sunlight.

NODE The place on the plant where a leaf attaches to the stem.

PERENNIAL PLANTS that live year after year, becoming dormant over winter.

PHOTOSYNTHESIS The process by which plants convert light, water and carbon dioxide into chemical energy.

PINCHING Removing part of the plant by 'pinching' it away from the stem or stalk, enabling it to grow fuller and bushier.

POTTING MIX Specialist potting medium for growing particular types of plants.

PROPAGATE The process of growing a new plant from seed or cutting.

PRUNE Removing unwanted parts of the plant to aid growth or improve aesthetics.

RE-POT Replacing the plant's pot, often with one that's larger in size.

ROOT-BOUND Occurs when a plant's roots have run out of space and are having trouble absorbing water and nutrients from the soil.

RUNNER An offshoot from the root or stem which can be removed and planted to create a clone of the mother plant.

SOAK To immerse a plant in water or allow water to flow freely through the soil and drainage holes.

SPECIES A sub-group of plants that share similar characteristics.

STEM The part of the plant where leaves and buds form. This is usually an elongated stalk above ground, but occasionally it forms below the soil line.

STRATIFICATION Treating seeds to simulate the natural conditions required for germination to take place.

SUCCULENT Plants originating from arid regions that can store water and therefore withstand droughts. All cacti are succulents.

TROPICAL Any plant originating from the tropics.

VARIETY A precisely defined group of plants from within a species.

INDEX

PICTURE CREDITS

Title page: Shutterstock.com

pp.6, 8, 9, 11, 16, 21, 25, 34, 35, 36, 37, 38, 39, 40, 41, 48, 49, 50, 52, 54-5, 56, 57, 64, 65, 66 (middle), 70, 75, 77, 81, 85, 86-87, 90, 91, 93, 96, 97, 98,99, 107, 108, 109, 110, 111, 112, 116, 119, 121, 122, 123, 124,125, 126, 127, 130, 132, 135, 137 Shutterstock.com

p.8 Sia_v/Shutterstock.com

p.13 Ton Tectonix/Getty Images

p.18 Kav777/Getty Images

p.23 Petrenkod/Getty Images

p.35 Proxyminder/Getty Images

p.17 Krichevtseva/Shutterstock.com

p.19, 20, 51 Severin Candrian on Unsplash

p.22 Darya Petrenko/Alamy Stock Photo

p.24 shenricks/Stockimo/Alamy Stock Photo

p.29 Annie Spratt on Unsplash

p.30-1 Mirrelley/Shutterstock.com

p.32 Bibadash/Shutterstock.com

p.34 Dmitrii Melnikov/Alamy Stock Photo

p.35 Todd Boland/Shutterstock

p.39 (middle) Fiona Smallwood on Unsplash

p.39 (bottom) Sarah Bronske on Unsplash

p.42-3 Walnut Bird/Shutterstock.com

p.44-5, 76 (right) Fir Mamat/Alamy Stock Photo

p.46-7 TorriPhoto/Getty Images

p.53 See D Jan/Getty Images

p.58-9 Wildlife GmbH/Alamy Stock Photo

p.60, 61 Tatyana Krymova/Shutterstock.com

p.65 Yvette Cardozo/Alamy Stock Photo

p.66 (top), 103 Tamara Kulikova/Alamy Stock Photo

p.66 (bottom) Olga Ionina/Alamy Stock Photo

p.67 Lois GoBe/Alamy Stock Photo

p.69 Anastasila Nastyna/Shutterstock.com

p.72-3 Nadia Grapes/Shutterstock.com

p.74 Stephanie Harvey on Unsplash

p.75 (left) Jay's Photo/Getty Images

p.76 Gina Easley/Stockimo/Alamy Stock Photo

p.78 Kari Shea on Unsplash

p.80 Alenka Karabanova/Shutterstock.com

p.88-9 Viktorija Reuta/Shutterstock.com

p.92 AY Images/Getty Images

p.94 Alexandra Grablewski/Getty Images

p.95 Susanna Barzaghi/Alamy Stock Photo

p.104-5 Guaxinim/Shutterstock.com

p.106 Dom Uccello/Shutterstock.com

p.113 Jure/Getty Images

p.115 (top) Undefined Undefined/Getty Images

p.115 (bottom) Julian Eales/Alamy Stock Photo

p.116 (top) Bhofack2/Getty Images

p.117 (top) Burke's Backyard/Alamy Stock Photo

p.117 (bottom) Ryan Quintal on Unsplashp

p.118 (top) Kmfdm1/Alamy Stock Photo

p.118 (bottom) Kcline/Getty Images

p.119 (bottom) Handmade Pictures/Getty Images

p.128-9 Anastasia Ultramarin/Getty Images

p.130 Sasimoto/Alamy Stock Vector

p.131 Veronika Ollinyk/Alamy Stock Vector

p.136 Dmitry Marchenko/Alamy Stock Photo